SEXUALITY AND EROTICISM AMONG MALES IN MOSLEM SOCIETIES

Arno Schmitt
Jehoeda Sofer
Editors

SOME ADVANCE REVIEWS

"A pioneering work in gay studies—the first book published on the theme. Moreover, it is a work of both eminent scholarship and good journalism. The social and political implications of homosexuality are made abundantly clear. The book is recommended to anyone interested in gay studies, the politics of sex and gender and in the Arab world."

Gert Hemka, PhD
Chair, Gay and Lesbian Studies
University of Amsterdam, The Netherlands

"We are only just beginning to gather significant amounts of reliable data about same-sex eroticism in other cultures, much less to conceptualize this data into genuine cross-cultural comparisons. The [chapters] in this book provide both insider and outsider perspectives on male-male sexuality in Muslim societies. These perspectives contribute significantly to an appreciation for both the differences and the similarities that exist, regarding homosexual acts and gender roles, among peoples of different cultures."

Walter L. Williams, PhD
Associate Professor of Anthropology
and the Study of Women and Men in Society
University of Southern California, Los Angeles

NOTES FOR PROFESSIONAL LIBRARIANS AND LIBRARY USERS

This is an original book title published by Harrington Park Press, an imprint of The Haworth Press, Inc. Unless otherwise noted in specific chapters with attribution, materials in this book have not been previously published elsewhere in any format or language.

CONSERVATION AND PRESERVATION NOTES

The paper used in this publication meets the minimum requirements of American National Standard for Information Sciences—Permanence of Paper for Printed Material, ANSI Z39.48-1984.

Sexuality and Eroticism Among Males in Moslem Societies

HAWORTH Gay & Lesbian Studies
John P. De Cecco, PhD
Editor-in-Chief

New, Recent, and Forthcoming Titles:

Gay Relationships edited by John De Cecco

Perverts by Official Order: The Campaign Against Homosexuals by the United States Navy by Lawrence R. Murphy

Bad Boys and Tough Tattoos: A Social History of the Tattoo with Gangs, Sailors, and Street-Corner Punks by Samuel M. Steward

Growing Up Gay in the South: Race, Gender, and Journeys of the Spirit by James T. Sears

Homosexuality and Sexuality: Dialogues of the Sexual Revolution, Volume I by Lawrence D. Mass

Homosexuality as Behavior and Identity: Dialogues of the Sexual Revolution, Volume II by Lawrence D. Mass

Understanding the Male Hustler by Samuel M. Steward

Sexuality and Eroticism Among Males in Moslem Societies edited by Arno Schmitt and Jehoeda Sofer

Men Who Beat the Men Who Love Them: Battered Gay Men and Domestic Violence by David Island and Patrick Letellier

Sexuality and Eroticism Among Males in Moslem Societies

Arno Schmitt
Jehoeda Sofer
Editors

Harrington Park Press
An Imprint of The Haworth Press, Inc.
New York • London • Norwood (Australia)

ISBN 0-918393-91-4

Published by

Harrington Park Press, an imprint of The Haworth Press, Inc., 10 Alice Street, Binghamton, NY 13904-1580

Cover design by Marshall Andrews.

Library of Congress Cataloging-in-Publication Data

Sexuality and eroticism among males in Moslem societies / Arno Schmitt, Jehoeda Sofer, editors.
p. cm.
Includes bibliographical references and index.
ISBN 0-918393-91-4 (pbk.)
1. Homosexuality, Male – Islamic countries. 2. Gay men – Islamic countries – Sexual behavior. 3. Sex – Religious aspects – Islam. I. Schmitt, Arno. II. Sofer, Jehoeda, 1944-1990.
HQ76.2.I74S49 1991
306.76'62'0917671 – dc20 91-2319
CIP

DEDICATED TO JEHOEDA SOFER
1944–1990

This book is dedicated to my co-editor and friend whose life was as rich in diversity and texture as the world in which we live.

Jehoeda Sofer, born into a Jewish family in the Moslem city of Baghdad, Iraq, grew up in a neighborhood of Oriental Jews in an Israel that perceived itself as a part of the West. Jehoeda viewed himself as an Arab Jew. He loved the land of Palestine/Israel and felt the awesome beauty of Jerusalem/Al Quds with never diminishing intensity.

Jehoeda dedicated his life to a deeper understanding of the culture, literature, and heritage of the peoples of the Middle East and to the dissemination of knowledge. He fought for the oppressed regardless of race, religion, sex, economic class, nationality, political beliefs, or sexual orientation.

After moving to Amsterdam, Jehoeda played a vital role in both the Dutch and international movements for gay and lesbian rights. He was an integral member of the *International Lesbian and Gay Association*, where he was especially involved with Third World concerns. Both in the Netherlands and in the Jewish communities of Europe and Israel, he was an active proponent for peace in the Middle East, striving for the reconciliation of Jews and Arabs.

As an author of numerous articles, Jehoeda greatly contributed to the better understanding of the underlying conflicts and possible solutions to the problems in the Middle East as well as for the oppressed. His many Palestinian friends learned through him that a Jew, a gay Jew at that, could fight for the freedom of Palestinians and Israelis and for peace between the states of Israel and Palestine.

He kept his dignity even into death. He chose to be buried as a Jew. Both the publishers and I regret that he was unable to see this book in print.

To my friend and colleague,

Arno Schmitt
Berlin, November 7, 1990

ABOUT THE EDITORS

Arno Schmitt studies Islamology at the Freie Universität in Berlin. He has recently compiled a bibliography of nearly 30,000 items on male-male sexuality and eroticism in Moslem society. He lives in Berlin.

Jehoeda Sofer (1944–1990) worked as a journalist in The Netherlands, where he was undertaking country-by-country research on legislation concerning sexual activities between males. He was a frequent contributor/editor to publications on homosexuality and on the Israeli-Palestinian conflict. He had been active since 1975 in the Dutch and the international lesbian and gay movement.

CONTENTS

Foreword

Until recently, "homosexuality" was seen as a minor part of our common history, the preserve of the prurient or the "special interest." Today, thanks largely to the efforts of lesbian and gay historians, we can see clearly its centrality: studying same-sex eroticism and relationships throws light on a whole culture, illuminates the complex ways of life within it, and above all informs us about the prevailing power relations around gender and sexuality. This book does just that for the Muslim societies it explores.

There is much that could be said concerning the rich material in this book. I would like to start, however, by looking a little more closely at that word "homosexuality" which I have put in quotation marks. It is a word we now take for granted as having a universal meaning. It implies a common psychological type, a common set of desires and sexual practices, and common meanings, which would allow lesbians and gay men to recognize one another across time, and across cultures. It suggests a truth about people's needs and personal characteristics which sets "homosexuals" apart, the eternally different.

The recent historical, sociological, and anthropological work suggests something different. We now know, for example, that the concept of "the homosexual" is of very recent origin. The term "homosexuality" itself was not invented until 1869, and the idea that homosexuals belonged to a common sexual species was largely an invention of sexology, the would-be science of sex, which developed in the West in the late 19th and early 20th centuries.

This does not mean, of course, that same-sex erotic activity did not exist before then. On the contrary, there is abundant evidence of it. The crucial point, however, is that it had different implications from the ones we now impute to it. To put it bluntly, homosexuality, like all forms of sexuality, has different meanings in different cultures—so much that it becomes difficult to find any common essence which links the different ways it is lived, apart that is, from the pure sexual activity itself.

On a world scale, however, historians have now begun to trace two great patterns by which different cultures have attempted to come to terms with same-sex activity. The pattern that by and large has predominated in the West until recently has associated male homosexuality with effeminancy. To have homosexual desires, to want to have relations with men, was to define yourself as almost a non-man. When the pioneer homosexual rights campaigners of the early part of this century spoke about homosexuals as belonging to the "third" or "intermediate" sex, they were trying to give some coherence to the idea that homosexuals were not properly men, nor yet quite women.

The other great pattern is the one this book shows to be predominant in the Muslim countries. It essentially allows, or at least condones, male same-sex activity under certain clearly defined limitations. Men may have sex with other males, without social obloquy, as long as they are the penetrators, and their partners are boys, or in some cases effeminate men (that is, just like the Western pattern, men who are not "real men"). There is, however, no concept of "the homosexual," except where it has been imported from the West, no notion of exclusive homosexuality, and no gay way of life.

Many Western gays, for a long time now, have traveled hopefully to the Muslim world and expected to find a sexual paradise. The reality is rather more complex. In the first place, the sexual priveleges allowed to men are largely at the expense of women, whose sexuality and social independence is tightly controlled. Secondly, those adult men who do not fit readily into prevailing notions of true manhood (that is, local men who are effeminate, or just want to lead an exclusively gay life, or Westerners themselves) are often looked down upon and despised.

But a third point is equally important, as this book brings out. Although there are many common elements that unite the Muslim countries from Morocco to Afghanistan, not least the religious culture, there are also many differences. The common elements derive from a long history of interaction, for much of that time as part of the same imperial system, from the empire of Alexander the Great to that of the Ottoman Turks. Many of the sexual mores in fact predate the rise of Islam, which itself condemns sodomy.

The differences derive from a number of factors: the degree to which Islamic Law is enforced, the impact of different Western colonial influences and legal systems, and the sheer impact of cultural variation within so vast an area.

This book does not, of course, pretend to capture all that variety. It does two things, however, rather well. First, it portrays very clearly the relationship between same-sex eroticism and the ideal of the man as penetrator. The result is to illuminate not only homosexuality, but a whole sexual culture. Secondly, it captures a sense of the Muslim countries in the process of rapid change. This takes many forms, from the anti-modernist and religious fundamentalism of Iran to the attempts in the cities of Turkey to develop a Western-style gay way of life, with all the difficulties that involves.

What we are seeing, in fact, is yet another phase of the ancient dialogue of the West and the East, sometimes confrontational, sometimes mutually beneficial. In the process the meanings of same-sex eroticism are likely to change. This book, like a photographic image, captures the sexual culture of the Muslim societies at a crucial moment. Only time will tell whether that culture will approximate more and more to the secularised Western model, or come increasingly under the sway of a new religious militancy. What can be said with some assurance is that it is unlikely to stay the same.

Jeffrey Weeks

Preface

Sexuality in Moslem society is surrounded by myths. Moslems are often seen as oversensuous, sexually cruel, perverted.

Modern Western opinion still abounds with prejudices about Eastern sexuality. On the one hand Islām is perceived as frighteningly anti-homosexual to the extent of threatening sodomites with death; on the other hand many gays believe all Moslems to be bisexual. The colony of Western homosexuals in Tangiers spread the saga of easily available boys and men.

Even gay scholars, on the search for examples of positive attitudes towards homosexuality, idealized Islamic society. John Boswell (in *Christianity, Social Tolerance and Homosexuality*, Chicago: University of Chicago Press, 1980) says that "most Muslim cultures have treated homosexuality with indifference, if not admiration" (p. 194) and that Islam generally has a "positive attitude toward gay sexuality" (p. 198). No evidence is given to support these statements. Michel Foucault classified Islam in the first volume of his *Histoire de la Sexualité* as one of the societies with an "ars erotica," a title of honor he later repealed. Fascination has been replaced by disillusionment in theory and in practice.

An inducement for this publication was the discussion in the European gay movement on behavior towards Turkish and Arab immigrants, and towards sex tourism in the Middle East, a discussion focusing on the "racist" attitudes of white gays, neglecting the cultural factors on the "colored" side. This is partly due to the lack of good information about sexuality in Moslem society.

Since Sir Richard Francis Burton's famous Terminal Essay to his translation of Alf Leila wa Laila (*The Book of Thousand Nights and a Night*, Benares: Kamasutra Soc., 1885 – 10 vols. plus 6 suppl.) – often reprinted, for example, as *Anthropological Notes on the Sotadic Zone* (New York: Falstaff, 1971) – no major study on male-

male sexuality and eroticism in Moslem society has been published in English. Our publication is the first larger work about sexuality and eroticism between males in Moslem society.

There was no "orientalist" work dedicated to the subject until 1977 when the prestigious *Encyclopédie de l'Islam* (Paris) and the *Encyclopaedia of Islam* (Leiden) published an article titled "Liwat," by the Parisian professor Charles Pellat. It is included in this book (supplemented with notes by Arno Schmitt).

This collection is aimed at anybody interested in "gay studies," especially anthropologists, orientalists, historians, students of comparative law, and sexologists. It should be of benefit to anybody in contact with Arabs, Turks, or Persians—be it as a tourist in Moslem countries, a social worker "in charge" of immigrants, or just as a friend of an immigrant. The articles vary from straightforward narrative to analytical essay, from plain description to academic treatise.

Please take note: we restrict ourselves to the geographical core of Islam. That includes the whole Arab world, plus Turkey, Iran, and Afghanistan; a belt of territory stretching from Mauritania to Uzbekistan. The Islamic societies in the Indian subcontinent, East Asia, and Sub-Saharan Africa are beyond the scope of this book, as those societies still draw heavily on their pre-Islamic cultures.

This book only treats sexuality and eroticism between males. The world of women in Islamic society is very closed. Little comes out into the open. Entry into the women's world for men is next to impossible. Research into this subject by female anthropologists has hardly begun.

We would like to thank all who helped us in realizing this book. To mention just a few: Anke von Kügelgen, Debbie Sofer, Gerd Hekma, Tom Morrison, Jack Huberman, Nick Perrenet and the translators of the various chapters who carried out their work voluntarily, and The Stichting Steunfonds Roze Front for the loan it granted us to get a number of chores done in the preliminary stage.

Arno Schmitt
Jehoeda Sofer

Acknowledgments

© for *An Italian in Morocco* by Gianni De Martino (first published in Italian in *babilonia*, Milano, 1983, 1986). © for English version by Arno Schmitt.

© for *Moroccan Boys and Sex* by Andreas Eppink (first published in Dutch as part of A. Eppink's PhD thesis, 1977). © for English version by Arno Schmitt.

© for *Among Syrian Men* by Gary B. MacDonald (first published as "Born to Lose" in *The Body Politic*, Toronto, June 1984).

© for *Intimate Look of the Iranian Male* by Jerry Zarit (first published in *GPU-News*, Milwaukee, October 1979).

© for *The Persian Boy Today* by David Reed (first published in *Christopher Street*, August 1978).

© for *Tehran: Dangerous Love* (Hélène Kafi) by Gai Pied Hebdo (first published in *gai pied hebdo*, 190: September 10, 1985). © for English version by Arno Schmitt.

© for *Turkey on the Brink of Modernity* by Mehmet Ümit Necef (first published in Danish in *pan*, Copenhagen, March 1985). © for English version by Arno Schmitt.

© for *Transvestites and Transsexuals in Turkey* by Thijs Janssen.

© for *Arab Men in Paris* by Dominique Robert (first published in *gai pied hebdo*, 77: September 7, 1983).

© for *liwāt* by *Encyclopaedia of Islam*, Brill, Leiden, 1983.

© for *Not-So-Gay Life in Karachi* by Badruddin Khan and Stephen O. Murray (first published in the *Society of Lesbian and Gay Anthropologists' Newsletter*, 12:1, February 1990).

© for *Islam* by Maarten Schild by Wayne R. Dynes (first published in *Encyclopedia of Homosexuality,* Garland, 1990).

PRONUNCIATION AND TRANSLITERATION

a, i, u are pronounced as in Italian or German
a as in French 'mal,' quality like in 'large,' but shorter
i as in 'sit,' 'this'
u as in 'book'
ā, ī, ū are longer vowels as in (large, glass; three, keen; soon, moon)
b, d, f, h, k, l, m, n, s, t, w, y, z as in English—but note that h is always audible
ḏ (= dh) voiced th as in 'the,' 'this'
ṯ (= th) voiceless th as in 'think,' 'thing'
ǧ (= j) voiced g as in 'gem,' 'George,' 'jam'
ġ (= gh) gargling sound almost like the French r—Grasséyé
r rolled r
ḥ strongly guttural h produced by strong expulsion of air from the chest. It should not be confused with:
ẖ (= kh) guttural ch, kh as in the Scottish 'loch' and German 'Bach'
š (= sh) as English sh, German sch, French ch, Hungarian s
q k-sound produced from the back of the throat
ṣ, ḍ, ṭ, ẓ emphatic sounds corresponding with s, d, t, z. In pronouncing them, the tongue is pressed against the edge of the upper teeth, and then withdrawn forcefully.
' glottal stop or spiritus lenis of Greek, the breathing necessary in English to begin a sentence, whose first Latin letter is a vowel: "Is that so?" In the middle of the word it involves a short pause as in "co-op."
' very strong guttural produced by compression of the throat and expulsion of breath

Spelling of Modern Turkish

ş = sh, š
ç = č = tš = tsh
c = j = ǧ = dsh
h = h (stands for ẖ as well)
j like in French: journal
ı dull i similar to 'first,' 'word,' 'under,' 'ago'
ğ stands for ġ, either not pronounced or like j, or voiced ẖ

Different Approaches to Male-Male Sexuality/Eroticism from Morocco to Usbekistān

Arno Schmitt

ANTHROPO-GEOGRAPHY

The articles in this book only deal with the central lands of Islām: the Arab speaking countries plus Irān and Turkey.

Subsaharan Africa, India, and Southeast Asia are relative newcomers to Islām, and have developed quite different civilisations. It is no coincidence that the core area of Islām covers the empire of Alexander the Great (plus Northwest Africa) or the southern Imperium Romanum plus Irān.

Our interest is not primarily directed toward 'good Muslims' but toward members of the Islāmic civilisation—which include quite a lot of Christians, Jews, and nonbelievers.

Incidentally, neither Muslim civilisation nor religion grew in the desert: Mecca was a mercantile city, Medina an agricultural oasis, and classical Islām was shaped in the towns of Syria and Mesopotamia.

The Islāmic civilisation is as Hellenistic as the Byzantine is and at least as much as western medieval Christian civilisation was. The so-called Arabs just kept much of the Hellenistic behavior and beliefs of their Aramaic-, Coptic-, or Greek-speaking parents. They learnt some of their theories by studying Greek texts, e.g., the medical belief that a man who likes to be fucked has in his ass the end of a nerve that normally ends in the penis. Also the medical belief, that the sex of a child is determined by "leftness vs. rightness": whether the semen is produced in the left or right testicle, whether the ovum is produced in the left or right ovary, and whether it nests in the left or right side of the womb. If all three factors are 'right' the child is a masculine male attracted by females; if all three factors are 'left,' the child is a normal female. Masculine women, transvestites, male-loving men, and other 'abnormalities' develop whenever the factors are part 'left,' part 'right.'[1]

The idea that pederasty is absent from peasants and nomadic peoples because a boy can learn everything he needs to know from his father, but that people of high civilisation require the erotic attraction of boys in order to motivate experienced men to teach boys lovingly[2] is of Greek origin.

Although the whole area is one cultural continent and one geographical unit (the winter rain zone of the Old World desert belt) characterised inter alia by the interplay between city dwellers, villagers, and nomads, due to geography and history there are great differences between different countries.

PSYCHOLOGY

From a psychoanalytical[3] constructionist[4] point of view it is not possible to take homosexuality as a starting point and study what forms it takes in different societies. The proper approach is to study the upbringing of boys, the way they are formed by the behavior and attitudes of people around them and then the behavior of youths and grown-up men.

When thus studying the development of oriental boys from the original amorphous sexuality to the socially formed sexuality of adulthood, we discover many common points between classic Hellas and the central lands of Islām: In both civilisations there is a strong separation between the domestic sphere of women and children and the public sphere of men.

This separation is not a matter of 'separate but equal' as Muslim apologists want us to believe. Men consider themselves to be stronger physically, intellectually, and morally, and to be able to control instinct and emotion—unlike women, children, slaves, serfs, eunuchs, barbarians, hermaphrodites, and transvestites.[5]

All of these groups and non-Muslims are discriminated against—in the economy, in ritual, in law, in the political sphere, as well as in matters of sex. It is the right of men to penetrate and their duty to lie on top.[6] Sodomisation of one's own slaves or of a Christian is not only sanctioned by public opinion, but by some jurists as well.[7]

To make sure that the wife is indeed inferior to her husband, one sees to it that the wife's family is neither economically nor socially superior to the husband's (this is similar to the practice of ancient Greece) (*kafāʾa*). Another way to ensure inferiority is through age: normally the wife is younger than the husband and often considerably so.

These privileges were justified by male superiority, but in reality they created this superiority.

The primary socialisation in the female-domestic sphere causes the boy to identify himself first with women—not unlike in classical Greece.[8] For his mother the little boy functions already as a man.

The rupture (often abrupt) with the domestic sphere and the passing into the phallic public sphere,[9] in which the boy has to "stand his ground" (but at the same time to bow in front of his father and other men in positions of power and respect[10]) allows for only a precarious male identity. This uncertainty is often hidden under macho behavior. The desire to be fucked, and the desire to be taken care of become subconsciously transformed into the wish to sodomise and to appear invulnerable. The grown man remains a non-man in relation to his father.[11]

A last point: the difference between the first-born and his younger brothers. The first boy is of tantamount importance to his mother. His mere existence changes her value in the eyes of society, he gets most love and attention and there is nobody above him but his father. The situation of the younger boys can be quite different.

So it is not surprising that I never met a first-born youth willing to take the submissive position of being penetrated, whereas many younger brothers viewed it as inevitable.

SOCIOLINGUISTICS I

Language and reality influence each other. Language is not only a reflection of reality as it is; it is not simply a mirror of what is the case, of things, relations, and actions. It shapes our perception of the world; it creates our reality. The language of a social group betrays much about its being and thinking.

Our language makes us see whites and blacks where 'in reality' there are only different shades of porcine pink, ivory, peanut, beech-wood, bronze with olive or yellow blended in, coffee, ebony, and hazelnut.

Our language makes us see homosexuals, where 'in reality' there are only men and women who perform sexual acts of a thousand different kinds, which can be classed according to hundreds of criteria, such as:

—number of people involved
—their ages
—their religions
—their ethnic groups
—their sex
—the place of the act
—the length of courting
—the roles love, violence, money, and social pressure play in bringing about the pairing
—the length of the act
—the physical technique of the act.

To phrase the central point in the philosophical language espoused by John Boswell in his *Revolutions, Universals and Sexual Categories*[12]*: universalia non realia, sula nomina sunt*; or in our case: there are no homosexuals independent of language, social perception, and expectations. Language does not merely label people without influencing them. Once homosexuals exist in the minds of people, once there are people who perceive themselves as homosexuals, there are homosexuals. Once there is a role of 'homosexual,' and some people choose this role or are forced into it, there are homosexuals.

But in the societies of North Africa and Southwest Asia there are no homosexuals, there is no word meaning homosexual, there is no such concept in people's minds.

The exception to the rule only confirms my thesis: during recent years something approaching a gay community grew in Turkey and during this time the Turkish word-by-word translation of homo-sex-uál-ity, *eş-cins-el-lik*, became current, and it is losing the old meaning of 'feminine man who gets buggered.'

SEXOLOGY

So if we disregard for the time being the newest development and regard the situation as it was for most of the Islāmic period, we find: In the societies of Muslim North Africa and Southwest Asia male-male sexuality plays an important role. But in these societies there are no "homosexuals"—there is no word for "homosexuality"—the concept is completely unfamiliar. There are no heterosexuals either.

Pederasty

For North Africans and Southwest Asians it is self-evident that men like to penetrate all kinds of beings. It is understandable that some men prefer boys to women.

That all men were susceptible to boyish beauty was taken for granted. Many would fall in love with boys. Many would desire sex with them and some would do it. The Hanbalite[13] jurisconsult Ibn al-Ǧauzī (died 597/1200[14]) wrote: "He who claims that he experiences no desire [when looking at beautiful boys or youth] is a liar, and if we could believe him, he would be an animal, not a human being."[15]

But desiring is not doing. And many a devout Muslim will have resisted and taken comfort in the Prophet's saying "Who passionately loves and remains chaste, is a martyr," i.e., he goes directly to heaven.

I personally would not call this sensitivity to boyish beauty, so often expressed in the high-brow poetry, homosexual. "In these instances . . . as in many others, the sexual object is not someone of the same sex, but someone who combines the character of both sexes" or—we might add—lacks characteristics of both sexes.[16]

It is easy to impress boys—in this respect they are similar to women, who have less experience in and less knowledge of the world than men. On the other hand boys are less strange to men than women—after all, the feelings of a boy were once one's own.

Sodomy Among Adult Males

Some boys who like to get fucked go on allowing men to bugger them. If done discreetly and if the fuckee marries and begets children, nobody cares. But there were always some who shunned women: they became dancers, singers, prostitutes.[17] In rural Morocco some fathers still sacrifice a boy not strong enough for agricultural labor to this craft.[18] In (modern) cities it is possible to go with men, to play the passive role, without making that one's profession, without making 'fuckee' one's only identity.

Whereas love of boys is natural to most North Africans and Southwest Asians, and it is known that some biological men like being fucked, it is completely incomprehensible to them that a man could prefer to sodomise adult males. Equally strange is the idea that a man could both sodomise and be sodomised by the same man. Whenever such things happen, it is best not to talk about them. But if one talks about them, it is mostly in order to recreate a fiction of a 'man' and a 'less-man': one who likes fuck and one who suffers sodomisation to please a friend.

I am not saying that men never take turns in fucking each other. I am saying that there is no social role of male-wants-to-fuck-male-and-wants-to-get-fucked-by-another-male, neither a tolerated role nor a condemned role, neither a pitied role nor the role of a psychologically ill person, neither a nonconformist role nor a defiant one of a self-conscious minority—although we find traces of the latter in medieval folk literature.

So when a MAN gets fucked one forgets it or it was due to alcohol, or he pretends not to have enjoyed it.

SOCIOLOGY OF CULTURAL INTERACTION

I repeat: the most normal thing is fucking boys. For the man, the buggerer, it is perfectly normal, if he is married and a father.

For the boy it is best to do it for extra-sexual benefits: gifts, favours, help from a well placed man, and—if he is poor—even for money. But he must stop at about the age of 16. The longer he continues, the quicker he gives in to advances, the worse for his reputation.

A man should not allow others to bugger him. Otherwise he loses his name, his honor, that is if others know it and are known to know. The decisive line is not between the act kept secret and the act known by many, but between only talking behind one's back and saying it in your presence, between rumors and public knowledge. There is always room for manoeuvre, you can always ignore what everybody knows. As long as nobody draws public attention to something everybody knows, one ignores what might disrupt important social relations.

There is a clear rule: You cannot be fucked. But what this really comes down to is: Saying of somebody that he has been fucked disturbs social relations.

The closing of the eyes is much easier when the man in question 'goes with' girls as well or, even better, is married; "only someone who can't fuck would allow others to fuck him" goes the saying.

Let me relate a story which happened around 1970 in a town on the Somali coast: "Ahmed is a young man who went to Saudi Arabia, where he gathered some basic Islāmic knowledge. When he returned home, he helped his father in teaching the Qur'ān to the young children. One day a [descendent Muḥammad] came to the mosque and tried to have sexual relations with one of the boys inside the mosque. The boy escaped and told his teacher, [who] felt bad for two reasons. First, homosexuality is against Islām as he understood it. Second, the mosque is the 'house of God' and, for that reason, the purest place. He went to the [descendent Muḥammad] and told him to get out of the mosque, and not to come back again. The people did not agree with [Ahmed's] behavior, and they stopped sending their children to his lessons. . . . The [descendent Muḥammad] declared that Ahmed, being trained in Saudi Arabia . . . had lost faith and had to be expelled from that mosque. [Ahmed had to leave town] for Mombasa to work as a porter in the market."[19]

Not so much getting fucked as enjoying it is considered bad: to show that one likes it increases the stigma.

If you suffer the penetration more or less, because you get something in return, or because you were forced to do it, it is bad. But to enjoy it is worse.

But there is a small problem with that: to most Muslims anal lust is not really unnatural. One has to avoid getting buggered precisely in order not to acquire a taste for it and thus become addicted. It is like an infectious disease: once infected it is difficult to get rid of it. Men stop getting fucked at the age of 15 or 16 and "forget" that they allowed/suffered/enjoyed it earlier.

In spite of all this activity I say there are no "homosexuals" and there is no (indigenous) word for "homosexuality."

SOCIOLINGUISTICS II

In classical Arabic there was no word meaning homosexuality; the translations given in modern dictionaries are either recently coined literal translations of 'homosexuality' or simply wrong.

In the first category I want to mention *al-ğinsīya al-mitlīya* (same-sex-uality), *al-mail al-ğins al-mumātil* (inclination toward the same sex) and *ištihā' al-mumātil* (carnal passion for the same). All the terms are new and, although 'passively' understood by most educated Arabs, are hardly part of the 'active' vocabulary even of physicians or sociologists.[20]

The most prominent word in the 'wrong category' is '*liwāṭ*.' Many dictionaries translate it as 'homosexuality.' Since many people—including Arabs—rely on the dictionaries, so that the word might indeed one day acquire the meaning of homosexuality, let me go back to the old Arabic-Arabic dictionaries. They explain the word *liwāṭ* as *ʿamal qaum lūṭ*, i.e., 'the doings of Loth's people,' which reveals at once that an activity is meant, not an inclination, nor a character trait or a genetic 'default.' To find out what *liwāṭ* precisely means we can consult the *Qur'ān* to see what it tells about 'the doings of Loth's people' (VII 80-84; IX 70; XI 77-81; XV 58-77; XXI 74,75; XXII 43; XXVI 160-175; XXVII 54-59; XXIX 28-35; XXXVII 133-136; XXXVIII 17; L 13; LIII 53; LIV 33-40). We can also study all kinds of Arabic texts where the word, or other words from the same root, occur.

But let me first explain something about the structure of Arabic words and explore the 'vocabulary of male-male sex and eroticism' more widely.

All (regular) words have a root of three consonants; they carry the main meaning. Vowels, (and sometimes) prefixes, suffixes, and doubling of the middle consonant add the necessary precision.

k t b	denotes the idea of 'writing' (but is no word and has no sound)
k*a***t***a***b***a*	he wrote (the most simple form of the verb)
k*i***t***ā***b**	something written, a book
k*u***t***tayi***b**	a booklet
k*ā***t***i***b**	a scribe
k*u***t***u***b***ī*	a bookseller
k*u***t***ā***b**	a school for writing (and reading the *Qur'ān)*
k*i***t***ā***b***a*	(act of) writing
*ma***kt***a***b**	place for writing, office
*mi***kt***ā***b**	typewriter
*i***kt***ita***b**	registration
*a***kt***a***b***a*	to make write = to dictate
k*ā***t***a***b***a*	to exchange letters
*ta***k***ā***t***a***b***a*	to write to each other

The forms are not just sound modifications of the basic root, to which meaning can be given ad libidum. They themselves carry some information: *ma* at the beginning (followed by the first two consonants without vowel between them and then by a short vowel) implies place:

masǧid, a place to prostate → Mosque
maẖzan, a place to store something → magazine

Leading *ta* and long second vowel implies reciprocity:

takātaba to write to each other
tasāfaḥa to whore with each other

Now, it is interesting to look out for words like "to make love with each other," "to fuck each other," "to suck each other": All I found was *taʿāšara* "to be intimate with each other, to live together" (not implying sex), and *bāšara* "to touch each other, to have sexual intercourse" (although without *ta* here denoting reciprocity, like *kātaba* 'to exchange letters' and *ǧāmaʿa* 'to have (hetero-)sexual intercourse'), and finally *talāʿba* "to play with each other, to have sexual games—not foreplay—but 'innocent' games, i.e., sex without penetration."

But most of the Arabic synonyms for 'to fuck' have no form of reciprocity. Let me give you a list of some of them; I find their literal meaning rather revealing:

rakaba	to ride (lit.: he rode);
ḍaraba	to beat ≈ *darraba* = to tame
dahala	to penetrate, introduce
aulaǧa	to insert
walaǧa	to enter, to penetrate
waqaba	to put into a hole
ṯaqaba	to pierce
waṭiʾa	to set foot on, to mount (a horse), to cover, to fuck
iftaraša	to sleep with, to spread ≈ *farraša* to cover, to pave (common idea: to lie over, to lie on top)
safida +	*sāfada* to beat, to mount, to cover, to cohabit
≈	*saffada* to pierce, to put on a skewer
qaraʿa	to knock, rap, hit, bump, beat
dāra ʿala	to turn around
wāqaʿa	to attack, to fuck ≈ *auqaʿa* = to bring down
nāka	to fuck
nahaka	to insult, to abuse, to rape
qahara	to overpower
ʿafaǧa	to bugger (enculer) ← *ʿafǧ* = duodenium

Terms designating the buggerer are:

fāʿil	the active, the doer
ṣāniʿ	the doer, the worker, the laborer
ʿalā	the one on top
dabbāb	the crawler (over somebody)

A common Persian word is *ġulām-pāre*; *ġulām* is Arabic and means 'boy,' *pāre* could mean 'one who tears apart' (this word entered Osmanli as *kulāmpāre*, from which modern Turkish derived *kullanpara* 'someone who takes money' and the modern Greek *kolobarás* 'enterer of the anus').

Another Persian word has completely different connotations: *šāhid-bazī*; *šāhid* is Arabic and means originally 'witness' and 'witness for his faith = martyr'; in *Ṣūfī* parlance it acquired the sense of 'witness of God's beautiful creation' being applied to boys so beautiful that only God could have created them.

In Cairene slang *bitūl ʿiyāl* 'someone having to do with children' is used for any *lūṭī*/buggerer, irrespective whether he fucks boys or men.

In the slang of circles of men who like to be fucked, they refer to themselves as 'woman' (in Cairo: *kudyana*[21]) and to the buggerer as 'man' (Cairo: *barġal*, generally: *rağel*).

The Turkish word *keskin* 'buggerer' stands for 'sharp, strong, active, penetrating.'

All these words refer either to an action or a preference, not to a character trait setting the *lūṭī*, the *šāhid-bazī* apart from other men.

That married men prefer to fuck boys is considered to be of no greater significance than the preference for classical music over popular styles, or wheat bread over durra loaves. This is not the case for most words designating the buggered:

mafʿūl	the passive
asfal	the one underneath
madbūb ʿalaihi	somebody crawled over by someone
malūṭ bihi	buggered one
manyak	the fucked one (means in modern Turkish: crazy, fool)

The Turks use *siktiren* 'someone who lets others fuck him.' *Maʾbūn* somebody who wants to be fucked; from this root in Turkish: *ibne* 'needs to be fucked'—and in Persian: *obnai*. Persian has a particularly telling expression:

koni	arse, asshole (in Turkish *pušt*—derived from another Persian word for arsehole)

In Arabic the word *ḥulāq* 'pathological sexual arousability of the anus' (and *ḥalaqī* 'somebody having a pathological desire to get buggered') shows an etymological connection to "anus."

Aḥmad at-Tīfāšī (d. 651/1253) speaks of a man who gets buggered as *baġā*; normally *baġā* could mean 'prostituting himself' or 'desiring strongly.'

In modern Persian *šarmūt* '(male) whore' is common for the buggered one.

The Arabic word '*ġulām*''s first meaning is 'boy,' the second 'slave,' the third 'catamite'—similarly the Turkish *oğlan* means both 'boy' and 'someone who gets fucked.'

Ḥawal, which first designated a professional dancer in women's clothes, is now used for 'sissies.' It is only one of several words which underwent this transformation of meaning (another one being *ālatī*). And there are cases of the reverse: *muhannat* is from the same root as the words for 'hermaphrodite'; it acquired the meaning 'dancer in womanish dress.' Even today there are *hanit*s in Oman going about their business of prostitution.[22]

The Arabic word for buggerer, *lūṭī*, lost in Persian its 'positive' meaning and stood both for masculine hooligans, wrestlers, ruffians, and for merrymakers, fools, showmen, dancers, singers, and musicians.

The word *amrad* meaning 'beardless youth' then 'dancer in women's clothes' quickly acquired the meaning of 'buggered boy' (in Turkish it can denote any buggered man, and carries the meanings of "stupid, crafty, cowardly, spiritless, ignoble, infamous, disgraced"[23]).

The words most common in Northwest Africa are:

ʿaṭaʾī	giver (of his arse)
ḥassās	sensitive, soft one[24]
mamḥūn	afflicted, addicted (to being buggered)
zāmel	a rather nice word; *zamīl* is colleague, being from the same root

All these words refer either to boys (not yet men) or to people of lower status (showmen, not equal, i.e., socially no-men) or to men who are sexually not men, but women (they get fucked).

Unlike the *lūṭī*s, who are normal men doing something many men do, the *maʾbūn*s are not real men, they do not perform, and they are somehow like women.

I think that this vocabulary reflects a sharp separation between penetrator and penetratee and a preoccupation with anal intercourse. Even a word that does not signify anal intercourse, *tafhīd*, betrays the tantamount importance of this one technique. *Tafhīd* is in scholarly English 'frictio inter fermores,' i.e., rubbing (of the penis) between the thighs. It is clearly a substitute for the real thing; if somebody stubbornly refuses to let the cock in, he gets nevertheless 'fucked' from behind, either between the buttocks or between the thighs.

One remark before I come to the promised explorations of the meaning of *liwāṭ*: I would not have given you this analysis of the words used in classical Arabic (and modern speech) if the contents of the old texts did not confirm the analysis of terms.[25] From questionnaires filled in by Moroccan boys and girls and from discussions with some of them, Andreas Eppink came to similar conclusions.[26]

THE MEANING OF LIWĀṬ

The root of *liwāṭ* is *l w ṭ (w* being a weak consonant can both 'disappear' and 'become' the vowel *u*). The verbs "doing *liwāṭ* (on)" are *lāṭa* (*bi*) and, sometimes, the corresponding Third Form *lāwaṭa* (*bi*).[27] Someone doing it, the *fāʿil*, is called *lūṭī, lāʾiṭ, mulāwiṭ* or *mutalauwiṭ*.

By the way: one should not speak of 'sodomy with' a boy. In Arabic it is *lāṭa bi,* not *lāṭa maʿ—maʿ* meaning 'together with, jointly' and *bi* meaning 'by means of, by, with the help of, through' like in *ba-bās* 'by bus,' *be-īd* 'with the hands.' So the preposition shows that one does *liwāṭ* not with a partner, but rather one uses him as an instrument (for enjoyment), one does *liwāṭ* on a boy, by means of a boy.

Someone upon whom *liwāṭ* is done, the *mafʿūl*, is called *malūṭ* (*bihi*).

The feminine form of *lūṭī*, *lūṭiya*, designates not a woman-*lūṭī* (as it should be, if *lūṭī* referred to 'someone behaving homosexually,'[28] but designates the action, is synonymous with *liwāṭ*, *liwāṭa*, and *mulāwaṭa*. Nowhere in the literature is a woman *lūṭīya* mentioned.

There are plenty of *aḥādīṯ*, sayings attributed to the prophet Muḥammad,[29] about *ʿamal qaum lūṭ* (i.e., 'the doing of the people of Sodom'); in most of them a *fāʿil* and a *mafʿūl (bihi)* are mentioned, or in the same sense an *aʿlā* (the one on top) and an *asfal* (the one underneath); in Imāmite (*šiʿite*) texts *lūṭī* and *malūṭ (bihi)* are used as well.

Consequently *liwāṭ* cannot refer to an action by one person by himself or a joint action by several 'equal' actors, but only to something done by someone to somebody else.

Occurrences in Juridical Texts

This 'one sided,' 'transitive' view explains an opinion held by the eminent jurist Abū Ḥanīfā, in the words of his disciple al-Kāsānī (d. 587/1191): "As to *liwāṭ* initiative is on one side only, it is not necessary at all on the side of the object."[30] Another Ḥanafite jurist, the Transoxanian al-Marġinānī (d. 592/1197), makes the same point in his *Hidayā*.[31]

Neither the *aḥādīṯ* nor the Sunnite jurists say precisely what a *fāʿil* or a *mafʿūl bihi* is; they presume that everybody knows.

A phrase by the Šāfiʿite an-Nawāwī (d. 676/1277), *wa dubr ḏakar wa unṯa*,[32] i.e., 'and the male and female anus,' shows that jurists consider sodomy upon a male person in the same context as sodomy upon a female person. The first sentence in the relevant chapter of al-Marġīnānī's *Hidāya* reads: "If a man enters a woman from the odious opening or commits *ʿamal qaum lūṭ*, it is no case of *ḥadd* [mandatory punishment]—according to Abū Ḥanīfa."[33]

In the same vein—even more clearly—al-Ḥaṣkafī (d. 1088/1677) writes in his *ad-Durr al-muhtār*: ". . . the fucking in the anus: both (Abū Yūsuf and Muḥ. aš-Šaibānī) said: Doing it with aliens [i.e., men not one's slaves and women not one's slaves nor one's wifes] is a case of *ḥadd*. Doing it with one's own slave or one's own woman slave or one's wife is, according to the consensus, a case of *ḥadd*. . . ."[34]

Another obvious quote is from the Ḥanbalites Ibn Qudāma (d. 620/1223) and his commentator ʿAbdarraḥmān ibn Ibrāhīm al-Maqdisī (d. 624/1227). Ibn Qudāma: "Whoever commits the abomination in vaginam vel anum of a woman not his property, or upon a boy (*ġulām*). . . ." Al-Maqdisī comments: "The forbidden fucking in anum is the abomination, wherefore God said to Lūṭ's people: 'Do you commit the abomination?' i.e., buggering in the arse of a man."[35]

A *ḥadīt* transmitted by Aḥmad ibn Ḥanbal and Abū Dā ʾūd aṭ-Ṭayālisī[36] shows that *liwāṭ* cannot only be committed upon men: *al-lūṭīya aṣ-ṣuġrā yaʿnī ar-rağul yaʾṭī imraʾtahu fī dubriha*

اللوطيّة الصغرى يعني الرجل يَأْطي إمرأته في دُبرِها

(the small sodomy that is a man fucking his wife in her anus).

Another 'proof' is by Masʿūd ibn ʿUmar at-Taftāzānī (d. 791/1389 or later); he writes in his *Šarḥ ʿala'l ʿAqāʾid an-Nasadīya*[37]: *wa fī'stiḥlālihi* ***al-liwāṭa bi'mraʾtihi*** *lā yukaffar ʿalā'l aṣaḥḥ*.

وفي استحآلِه اللواطة بِإمرأتهِ لاٌ يكفّر على الاصحّ

(to declare sodomy on one's wife as allowed is no heresy).

So far we can deduce the following definition: sodomy = pedicatio.[38] In most cases pedicatio upon boys is meant, sometimes pedicatio upon men, or upon women. (The expression *ʿamal qaum lūṭ* refers—as far as I see—never to sodomy upon women; for sodomy upon women *lūṭīya* or *liwāṭa* are normally used.)

In a broader sense *liwāṭ* can stand for 'fucking' between the thighs (*tafhīd*) or between the buttocks. The stories in at-Tifāsī's sex guide (see below) show that *tafhīd* is only a substitute for *liwāṭ* which the *lūṭī* actually desires.

Some moralists use *liwāṭ* in a broader sense; for example al-Ġazzālī (d. 505/1111) writes in his *Iḥyāʾ ʿUlūm ad-Dīn*[39] not only of "*liwāṭ* of doing," but of "*liwāṭ* of looking" and "*liwāṭ* of touching" as well. This is a metaphorical use of the word presupposing the 'normal' sense. These three kinds of *liwāṭ* should not be seen as being on an equal footing; al-Ġazzālī does not define looking at and touching boys as *liwāṭ*, he just wants to warn the reader who otherwise might lose his self control.[40]

Occurrences in Non-Juridical Texts

Some references from non-juridical texts of the Muslim Golden Age will dispel last doubts that the definition of *liwāṭ* as 'buggery—first of all upon boys and youth, but upon men and women as well' is correct.

In the tenth chapter of his *Rušd al-labīb ilā muʿāšarat al-ḥabīb* entitled *Fī tafḍīl al-ġilmān,* Ibn Falīta (d. 231/845) writes again and again of 'fucking' (*nīk*) of boys; it is obvious that buggery is meant. This becomes absolutely clear in the following one-and-a-half verses:

ṭāba'l liwāṭ fa-lūṭū aiyuha'l-ʿarab nīkū ġulāman . . .[41]

طاب اللواط فلوطوا أيُها العرب ... ✻ ... نيكوا غلامَ ...

Buggery is good for you, oh, Arabs, bugger! fuck a boy . . .

The second part of the *Nuzhat al-albāb* by the Tunisian *qāḍī*, physician and mineralogist Abū'l ʿAbbās Aḥmad ibn Yūsuf at-Tifāšī (d. 651/1253)[42] confirms that *liwāṭ* refers to buggery.

If proof is needed that *liwāṭ* is not only different from homosexuality (an act, not a character trait; a deed, not an inclination), that it is not only narrower in regard to persons (it excludes female-female sex), and in regard to sexual techniques (fellatio, mutual masturbation, frictio inter abdomina are not *liwāṭ*), but that it is broader in another respect (it covers buggery 'against' or upon women), poetry offers an excellent example. Abū Nūwās (d. around 810) writes:

ʿalaiya ʿain^{un} wa-udn^{un} min mudakkara^{tin}
mamṣūla^{tun} bi-hawā'l lūṭī wa'l ġazil,[43]

عَليَّ عَينٌ وأذنٌ مِن مُذَكَّرةٍ ✻ مَمصُولَةٌ بِهَوَى اللوطيّ والغَزِلِ

translated by E. Wagner as follows[44]: “Mich hält ein bewachendes Auge und Ohr von einem Knabenmädchen ab, das mit Päderasten und Mädchen-liebhabern in Beziehung steht.” Roughly translated into English: An eye and an ear (are guarding) against my (coming together with) a girl in boy’s attire, whom both lovers of boys and lovers of girls desire.

Using a synonym to *mudakkara, ġulāmīya,*[45] he wrote an *ʿağuz* (second part of a verse) *taṣluḥu li'l lūṭī wa'z zānī* (she is fit for both *lūṭī* and *zānī*).

The first part, the *Ṣadr*, runs in the *Dīwān*[46]:

maṭmūmat aš-šaʿr ġulāmīya

مَطمومة الشعر غُلاميّة ✹ تَصْلُحُ لِلوطي والزاني

and in *Alf Laila wa Laila*[47]:

mamšūqahat al-ḫaṣr ġulāmīya

مَمشوقَة الخَصرِ غُلاميّة ✹ تَصْلُحُ لِلوطي والزاني

Slightly varied this verse is part of the most famous poem of this most famous poet of the Arabs[48]:

min kaffi dāti ḥirin fī ziyy dī dakarin
lahā muḥibbāni lūṭīyun wa zannāʾu

مِنْ كَفِّ ذَاتِ حِرٍ في زِيِّ ذِيْ ذَكَرٍ ✹ لَهَا مُحِبّانِ لوطيٌّ وَزَنّاءُ

Burton translates[49]: “From hand of coynted lass begarbed like yarded lad, Wencher and Tribe of Lot alike enamouring.”[50]

So far we have found:

1. Only men engage in *liwāṭ*; both men and women can be ‘homosexuals,’

2. *liwāṭ* refers to an act; if homosexuality would indeed refer to an act, there should be words like "*to homosexual somebody" or "*someone homosexualed," and
3. *liwāṭ* refers to an act irrespective of the sex of the object; homosexuality refers to the object of desire (partner) irrespective of the sexual role and the technique.

'Homosexuality': Wrong Translation, or Just not Entirely Correct?

There is an explanation for this error: a European finds in an Arabic text a mention of an act, which he (guided by his language) names 'homosexuality,' and this act is named in the Arabic text "*liwāṭ*." So he thinks homosexuality and *liwāṭ* are the same.

But one cannot infer identity of notions from an identity (or overlapping) of the sets of designated things, i.e., things referred to by these notions.

The 'scholar' who renders *liwāṭ* as 'homosexuality' makes the same mistake as the Arab who came to Antwerp and translated "diamond merchant" with *'yahūdī'* (Jew), merely because all diamond merchants he encountered were Jewish.

To close the chapter on language I want to draw some conclusions from two cases of borrowing and use of 'European' words in modern Arabic.

First, in Northwest Africa we find an expression for 'someone who gets buggered' (synonymous with *ʿaṭai, zāmel*): *pédé*. This word—derived from "pédéraste"—denotes in French 'a homosexual' irrespective of his sexual practices. In the Arab cultural context the word and the European to whom it is applied become identified, both linguistically and socially, with the 'buggered one.' Since the French *pédé*'s main interest is a male partner, not a particular sexual role, he normally accepts being buggered, and becomes thus reduced to this role—if not in bed, at least in the talk about him.

Second, for one species of 'men doing it with men' I found only foreign words, suggesting that they were a rather rare species before the arrival of foreign explorers, traders, soldiers, and tourists, further suggesting a connection between influx of foreigners, foreign pattern of behavior, and foreign words. I refer to three borrowed words for someone taking both roles in anal intercourse: in Cairene slang such a man is called *dublifās* or *dubləfīs* (← double face); in Algiers they are named *crêpe* after a pancake baked on both sides; or after round phonograph records, *disque*, playable on both sides.

CONCLUDING REMARKS

As the male-male act—and this is buggering and buggering only—happens between a MAN and a NON-MAN, it would be absurd to group both under one category, to label them with one word—as absurd as calling both the robber and the robbed one 'criminals' and implying they are basically the same.

Literally *dabīb* means 'crawling.' It involves the outwitting or overpowering of somebody. Normally someone is sodomised under cover of darkness, drunkenness, or drugs (the *dabbāb* drugs his victim in order to go about his business without resistance). The sodomisation of a person who consents can also be called *dabīb*, provided it happens against the will or without the knowledge of the guardian of the victim (the boy's father, the slave's owner).[51]

Penetration gives expression to or establishes superiority. "Ibn al-Habbara (d. 504/1100) relates an incident witnessed by himself and other men of rank and learning at a party in the Dār al-Wizāra in Isfahan. Quiet had descended on the group when suddenly there was a cry for help. The guests looked up and saw with astonishment that the *adīb* Abū Ǧaʿfar al-Qaṣṣās was sexually assaulting the poet Abū al-Ḥasan ibn Ǧaʿfar al-Bandanīǧī who was old and blind. When he had finished, Abū Ǧaʿfar explained: 'I always wanted to bugger Abū'l ʿAlā 'al-Maʿarrī [an old, blind poet] because of his unbelief and his atheism, but I never had the opportunity, so when I saw you, a learned and blind old man, I buggered you on account of him.'"[52]

One of the reasons Europeans misunderstand oriental male-male sex relations is the different boundaries between normal and abnormal and between different concepts.

Whereas in post-medieval Europe love, sex, affection, intimacy, and marriage were thought of as going ideally together, they are strictly separated in the minds of the Muslim middle-class. Love was thought of as an often unfulfilled longing for a woman or a boy.

Another form of love was deep friendship between equals. This friendship between men should not be confused with *liwāṭ/ubna*, which is sex between unequals.

Because the behavior of Muslims today can be seen as a modification of older behavioural patterns, the study of male-male sexuality in Muslim society should start from old texts—although most of these reflect the viewpoint of the middle-class only. Study of modern texts, conversation, and encounters with them and observations of Arabs, Iranians, Turks help us to understand not only the modern behavior, but the old texts as well.

In general, concepts and ideas change more slowly than behavior, but sometimes new ideas and ideals are adopted without being put into practice. Economic and social changes (industrialisation, entry of women into the public sphere, decreasing influence of the three-generation-household), on the one hand, and the influence of western ideas (through colonial rule, tourists, media), on the other hand, bring with them a change in the relationship between men and women and consequently in the sexual relationship between males.

Tourism does two things: it makes sex with women easier (the young men get many of the tourist girls and women), so that the 16 to 30 year olds no longer depend on their younger cousins and neighbors; and, they will lean less heavily on the younger and more delicate boys of the quarter.

In the eyes of the orientals even many European male tourists appear to be feminine; their white, soft skin and polite urban behavior make them less virile. To bugger 'whites' is psychologically especially attractive because, on the one hand, they represent the rich, strong, exploiting West, and, on the other hand, they are strangers, i.e., weak and 'helpless.'

Normally the oriental youth or man gets paid for these 'services'—with cash, food, entry fees, or gifts. The tourist even offers the possibility of getting buggered without 'anybody' knowing about it.

In summary there are:

—male-male acts,
—transvestites,
—male-male prostitution, and
—pederasty.

But there is:

—no role for men preferring sex with other men independent of the sexual technique;
—no gay community;
—a strong wish for a helper, servant, and mother of one's children; and
—a feeling that what young men do among themselves is of no real concern to society, and that a little fucking here and there is nothing to make a fuss about.

NOTES

1. Ursuala Weisser, *Zeugung, Vererbung und pränatale Entwicklung in der Medizin des arabisch-islāmischen Mittelalters*, Erlangen: Hannelore Lueling, 1983, S.296-300.

2. Iḫwān aṣ-ṣaffā', *Rasā'l*.

3. "Psycho-analytic research is most decidedly opposed to any attempt at separating off homosexuals from the rest of mankind as a group of a special character. By studying sexual excitations other than those that are manifestly displayed, it has been found that all human beings are capable of making a homosexual object-choice and have in fact made one in their unconscious. . . . psycho-analysis considers that a choice of an object independently of its sex—freedom to range equally over male and female objects— . . . is the original basis from which, as a result of restriction in one direction or the other, both normal and inverted types develop. Thus from the point of view of psycho-analysis the exclusive sexual interest felt by men for women is also a problem that needs elucidating. . . ." Sigmund Freud, *Three Essays on Sexuality* in *Standard Edition of the Complete Psychological Works of S.F.* vol VII, London: Hogarth Press, 1953, pp. 145/6.

4. I.e., homosexuality is not an inborn essence of certain persons, but acquired. The two sides in this controversy are called by the essentialist John Boswell 'nominalist' and 'realist.' (Boswell, *Revolutions, Universals and Sexual Categories* in *Salmagundi* 58,59, 1982).

5. Cf. the interesting essay by A. Cheikh Moussa *Ğāḥiẓ et les eunuques* in Arabica XXXIX, 1982.

6. Naṣīr ad-Dīn Abū Ğaʿfar Muḥ. b. Muḥ. b. al-Ḥasan aṭ-Ṭūsī gives medical reasons for (*K. Albāb al-Bāhīya wa't Tarākīb as-Sulṭanīya*, Chapter 10).

7. Some Malikites according to Abū'l Maʿāli Muḥ. b. ʿUbaidallāh al-Ḥusainī, edited by Charles Schefer in *Chrestomathie Persane* I p. 154. In Ibn Falīta, *Rušd al-Labīb*, ed. Moh.Z. Djabri, p. 14 a *mu'addin*, who has sodomized a Christian boy invokes Qur'ān IX, 120 ". . . *wa la yaṭa'ūna mauṭi'an ya-ġīẓu al-kuffār wa lā yanālūna min ʿadūwin nailan* (*illā kutiba lahum bihi ʿamalun ṣāliḥun*)"; Richard Bell translated: "nor do they make any invasion, which rouses the anger of the unbelievers. . . , but a good deed is thereby written to their credit." Since *waṭi'a* means i.a. "to have intercourse with" rather than "making an invasion," the *mu'addin* could be right.

8. Philip E. Slater, *The Glory of Hera*, Boston: Beacon, 1969.

9. Cf. Tahar Ben Jelloun, *La plus haute des solitudes*, Paris: Seuil, 1977. Hichem Djait, *La Personalité et le devenir arabo-Islāmique*, Paris: Seuil, 1975.

10. Cf. Sādiq al-Aẓm, *Naqd ad-dati baʿd al-Hazīma*, Bairut, 1969.

11. Abdalwahhāb Bouhdiba, *The Child and the Mother in Arab-Muslim Society* in L. Carl Brown (ed.), *Psychological Dimensions* . . . , Princeton, 1977.

12. *Salmagundi* 58,59, 1982.

13. Soon after Muḥammad's death Islām splinted threefold, Sunna und Šiʿa being the major groups. Of the former four schools are important: the Hanbalite, the Hanafite, the Šafiʿite and the Malikite; of the latter three groups are worth mentioning: the Zaidīs, the Ismaʿilīs, and the biggest group, the Imāmīs or Ğaʿ-farites often simply called Šiʿites.

14. The first number refers—here and always—to the muslim year (*ḥiğrī*), the second to the common year (A.D.).

15. Cit. by James A. Bellamy: Sex and Society in Islamic Popular Literature in *Society and the Sexes in Medieval Islam* (ed. A. L. Sayyid-Marsot), Malibu: Udena, 1976. p. 37.

16. *Three Essays*, ibid. p. 114.

17. Cf. Thijs Janssen, and Jehoeda Sofer, *Testimonies from the Holy Land* . . . , and Unni Wikan *Behind the Veil*, Baltimore: Johns Hopkins University Press, 1982, pp. 168-183.

18. Personal communication by Kenneth L. Brown during a lecture in Berlin.

19. Abdulhamid az-Zain: *The Sacred Meadows*, without place: North Western Uni. Press, 1974. p. 171.

20. The Persian *ham ğins bāz* = 'same sex playing' seems to be used among educated Persians.

21. Everett K. Rowson: Cant and Argot in Cairo Colloquial Arabic in *The ARCE Newsletter* 122, 1983. pp. 13-24.

22. Unni Wikan: *Behind the Veil*, Baltimore: Johns Hopkins University Press, 1982. pp. 168-183.

23. Minoo S. Southgate: Men, Women and Boys in *Iranian Studies* XVII.4 (Aut. 1984) p. 434.

24. Tahar Ben Jelloun: *La plus haute des solitudes*, Paris: Editions du Seuil, 1977, ²1979. p. 74.

25. Arno Schmitt: *Vorlesung . . .* in Schmitt, Ä.; DeMartino, G.: *Kleine Schriften . . .*, Berlin, 1985.

26. Andreas Eppink: *Familierelaties en Persoonlÿkheidsontwikkeling in Marokko*, Amsterdam, 1977—thesis; his article in this book is an English version of relevant chapter of his thesis.

27. The verb of the 5. Form, *talauwaṭa* occurring once in al-Ǧaḥiẓ's (d. 255/869) *Ḥayawān* ed. Hārūn, I p. 171; old standard edition: Qāhira, 1325, 1907, I p. 79) seems to be synonymous to *lāṭa bi* and not to imply reciprocity; the context (*ḫaṣī talauwaṭa wa yaṭlabu'l ġilmān*: the eunuch buggers and desires boys suggest this; *ġulām* being an often used terminus technicus for 'a willing boy before and after puberty' cannot refer to 'real men.' Note further that a *ḫaṣī* is "only" deprived of the power of his testicles, not of his penis—erections not impaired. Should *talauwaṭa* not be synonymous to the 1. Form, but mean 'to bugger with each other,' the eunuchs would not have to desire *ġilmān*, they could just *yatalauwaṭūn*

28. Maarten Schild: De Islam en homoseksueel gedrag in het Midden Osten in *Homologie* 6. 1983 p. 9—he writes in Dutch: "*luti*, degene die zich homoseksueel gedraagt." cf. his Ph.D. thesis: *De Citadel van Integriteit*, doctoraalscript, 1985.

29. The *aḥādīṯ* (sg. *ḥadīṯ*) are the second most important source of Muslim law (after the *Qurʾān*); there are thousands of them; therefore Muslim traditionalists tried to separate the true ones from the false *aḥādīṯ* (cf. the article *liwāṭ*).

30. *Badāʾiʿ aṣ-Ṣamāʾiʿ*. p. 41,51,52.

31. *Hidāya*, Calcutta, 1274/1818. p. 376; printed together with Ibn al-Humām: *Fatḥ al-Qadīr*, al-Qāhira: Maṭbaʿat al-kubrā al-amīrīya, 1316/1896. IV p. 150.

32. *Minhāǧ aṭ-Ṭalībīn*. ed. v.d. Berg, Batavia, 1884. III p. 211.

33. *Hidāya* ibid.

34. al-Haṣkafī: *ad-Durr* printed with Ibn ʿĀbidīn: *Radd al-muḥtār*, al-Qāhira, p. 27; Ibn ʿĀbidīn quotes Ibn al-Humām's phrase: "with his slave his female slave or his wife"—in Ibn al-Humām: *Fatḥ al-Qadīr*, al-Qāhira: Maṭbaʿat al-kubrā al-amīrīya, 1316/1898. p. 150.

35. Ibn Qudāma: *Kitāb al-ʿUmda*, al-Qāhira: Maṭbaʿat as-sa-lafīya, 1382/1962/3 (3rd ed.). p. 556; ibid. Maqdisī's commentary—'God's Word': *Qurʾān* XXIX 28.

36. Ibn Ḥanbal: *Musnad*, al-Qāhira, 1313/1894,5. II p. 182; Abū Dāʾūd: *Musnad* no. 2266, cit. by James A. Bellamy: Sex and Society in Islamic Popular Literature in *Society and the Sexes in Medieval Islam* (ed. A. L. Sayyid-Marsot), Malibu: Udena, 1976. p. 37.

37. al-Qāhira: ʿĪsā al-Bābī al-Ḥalabī, p. 149.4; translation: Earl Edgar Elder, *A Commentary on the Creed of Islam*, New York: Columbia University Press, 1950, p. 160.

38. The definition of pedicatio is 'penetratio per penem in anum' or in plain English 'buggery.'

39. al-Qāhira, 1352/1933. III p. 88.

40. Cf. Abū Sahl quoted by Ibn al-Ğauzī: *Damm al-hawā*, ed.: Muṣṭafā ʿAbdalwaḥīd, al-Qāhira: Dār al-Kutub al-Hadīta, 1381/1962. pp. 11,114,116 cit. engl. in J.N. Bell: *Love Theory in Later Hanbalite Islam*, Albany: State University New York, 1979. p. 21.

41. Ed. et trad. Moh. Zouher Djabri—basing himself on Ms. Gotha 2038—Diss. Med. Erlangen, 1968, p. arab 12 ≈ p. germ. 15; he translates both verbs prudishly '*beschlafen*': "Die Päderastie ist köstlich! Beschlaft die Knaben, oh Araber Beschlaft einen Knaben . . ."

42. Hs. Berlin Ahl. 6382. fol.46-135 (end of text).

43. Ew. Wagner: *Abū Nūwās*. p. 178; edition: Maṭbaʿat al-Lağna, 1378 and Wiesbaden: Fr. Steiner, 1958. p. 184.

44. Ew. Wagner: *Abū Nūwās*. p. 244.

45. Ew. Wagner: *Abū Nūwās*. p. 178; further synnonima: *rağulīya* and—of Persian origin—*zanmarda*.

46. *Bairūt*, 1382/1962. p. 627.

47. Ed. *MacNaughten, Calcutta: W. Thacker. II p. 462; translation: Burton V p. 161.*

48. *Ewald Wagner: Abū Nūwās*, Wiesbaden: Fr. Steiner. pp. 291,292; sowie *Alf Laila*, Calcutta, IV p. 715 (instead of *ğirin*, recte: *hirin*) and: Ibn Hallikān: *Wafayāt*, ed. Iḥsan ʿAbbās, I p. 223; de Slane translates 'only' into Latin, but at least correctly (I p. 205): "A manu muleris in vestimento hominis, cui duo amatores, paedico et scortator."

49. Translation Richard Burton, *The Book of the Thousand Nights and a Night*, Benares: Kamasutra Society, 1885-88 (10 vols), X p. 39.

50. Translation: Enno Littman, *Die Erzählungen aus Tausend und einer Nacht*, Wiesbaden: Insel, 1954, III p. 588: "Die schlanke Maid, die einem Knaben gleicht, Taugt für den Wüstling und den Ehebrecher."

51. Cf. Ğaubarī, *Kitāb al-Muhtār fī Kašf al-Asrār*, chapter 26; Ibn Falīta, *Rušd al-Labīb*, chapter 10; aṭ-Tifāšī, *Nuzhat al-Albāb*, chapter 9; Franz Rosenthal, *The Herb*, Leiden, 1971. p. 83.

52. James A. Bellamy: *Sex and Society in Islāmic Popular Literature* in *Society and the Sexes in Medieval Islām* (ed. A.L. Sayyid-Marsot), Malibu: Udena, 1976. p. 28, Ḏaḫā'ir, Dimašq, Atlas, 1964. p. 278.

An Italian in Morocco

Gianni De Martino
Arno Schmitt (translator)

The resurgence of Islamitic forces invigorates the idea of masculinity and the archaic structure of sexuality. The ruling class combines a legitimizing traditionalism with a proclaimed modernism in order to divert the revolutionary energy of the common people to an apathetic passivity or a primitive hedonism. Today everywhere in Morocco personal prestige and power are revered. Men seem to be entrapped by an excessive adoration of virility, identification with the father, hero worship, a cult of force and domination, contempt of everything weak, and disdain and fear of women.

The homosexual question has a peculiarly racist ring. Moroccans often tell you that homosexuality is only due to the foreigners and that 'scarcely a handful' of local young men engage in it—imitating the tourists. Later you find out that sodomy is very common in this society: one does it, but does not talk about it; men and boys make jokes and puns about it, allude to it, do it, but never talk about it in a serious manner.

This is due to the inaccessibility of women and to the character of relations between boys and men. It is common for a young man to prostitute himself for a movie ticket, a few nickels, or a small gift. Tourist homosexuality simply fits into this traditional pattern without changing it a lot. (A certain modernist/leftist discourse blames the Evil Capitalist West for everything and blames the tourist for exploiting the misery of the Third World—including its sexual misery. Tahar ben Jelloun, a Moroccan writer living in Paris, even called Morocco in one of his French poems a "child brothel for western tourists.")

DO NOT CONFUSE

There are these boys lounging about the boulevards hand-in-hand, underlining their jokes with gentle, tender gestures. Everyone has his own special intimate friend. They hang on each other's lips and eyes; they watch the faces, their hair, their hands. They pay each other compliments; they may tell somebody how beautiful he is. Some go as far as to write 'friendship letters'—(to me) virtually undistinguishable from love letters—but do not confuse them!

Then there are the boys between 9 and 17, who get fucked by their cousins, teachers, and neighbors—whether they like it or not (not necessarily by force, but by intimidation, by seduction, by making presents, or as a 'natural right'). These boys are called *zamel*.

By the age of 15 or 16 a *zamel* loses his admirers or he starts refusing advances: becomes a 'man,' i.e., he fucks boys and courts girls. Those continuing to get fucked are called *ḥassās*. Some become real swishing faggots with make-up and everything; they have their own little subculture: they appear as women, an image of an image, the imitation of the image the Maġribī (North African) has of a woman (distant, separated, idealized, and despised all at the same time).

Finally there is the great mass of men who like to fuck—girls, *ḥassās*es, married women, boys, tourists, and prostitutes alike.

NO SUPER-EGO

For those who want to get fucked, the problem is not a prohibiting internal super-ego, but external control: When it becomes known that you 'play the woman,' you become the object of ridicule, and the whole society is watching your every step; only in the Turkish bath is some action possible—disguised as a massage—as if by chance (no confusion possible with a gay sauna in pre-AIDS days). These *ḥammām*s are unknown to the tourists; they are the bath for the neighborhood, inaccessible to outsiders. In the big cities one or two *ḥammām*s are open to foreigners, for example the one near the el-Fna-Mosque in Marrakeš. Once it was closed down by police; an English tourist had died there in rather dubious circumstances—according to the death certificate of heart trouble; but it seems that he first got raped and robbed.

In Morocco, sex is an act of hygiene, a release of tension; it seems to be mere, pure sex undiluted by sentiments and emotions. In the West sexuality becomes somewhat trivial; it is a desire leaving you empty all the time—a desire lying in dialectical contradiction with the forbidden. In the Arabic-Islāmic world sexuality still has a holy, anti-modern character; it is divided into 'pure' and 'impure.' After the act the 'impure object' is thrown away like a dirty sheet—a quasi magical source of contamination. The Maġribian man eliminates the fucked one after the act; he denies all importance to the act and declares it to be free of sentiment. At once he rushes to the shower as if fulfilling the washing of Islāmic ritual.

GROUP HOMOSEXUALITY

There is a Moroccan peasant custom of (ceremonially) working and eating together; it is a sign of Islāmic solidarity and fraternity and is called *tuisa*.

When some boys band together to bugger somebody they talk of 'making a *tuisa*.' Here the *zamel* functions as a glue for the group; the desire does not have to be hidden, there is nothing shameful about it. It is a collective phallic appropriation of the arsehole and a 'sacrifice' of the *zamel* (who gets tricked into it by the promise of some reward, or just gets raped).

These practices are common, but not talked about. Islam disapproves both of the 'active' and the 'passive'; but people tend to accept the *lūṭī*, since he acts as a strong man subjugating a non-man . . . But to talk about it is something else, not because one feels guilty making it, but because it would be shameful to denounce somebody as having been fucked. Done discreetly one is able to pretend that nothing has happened.

Social control, or spying on each other, seems to make up for the weakness or even non-existence of a super-ego in individuals formed by the Arabo-Islāmic culture. In these lands external control is far more important than internalised prohibitions, feelings of guilt. . . .

THE STATUS OF WOMAN

Reproduction is still a very important aspect of sex—more important than eroticism. But the cardinal point of Islāmic sexuality is not the general practice of sodomy but the despising of women.

Women cannot freely transact their main social capital—their bodies. The separation of the sexes by veil, exclusion from public life, seclusion in the *ḥarim*, etc. is designed to protect it. A virgin is worth a lot; a deflowered woman passes for a used item, for a secondhand thing. Marriage is a social and commercial transaction. Subjected to apartheid, woman is a mysterious, almost unattainable, often idealized object. Simultaneously she is desired and feared precisely because she is unknown. Even where the separation is less rigorous (at work, on the beach) rarely is heterosexual 'love made.' If at all, petting, masturbation, and sodomy are practised. The vagina is excluded as a holy, forbidden part of the female body. Woman is the prime target of the desire (and fantasies) of the Moroccan. The diverting to the ass, just to release tensions, is something different from 'homosexuality' as understood in the West.

For a Moroccan to go to bed with a man presents no problem of sexual identity. Getting fucked does.

We in the West lost this simplicity during a long historical process in which the restraint and controlled manners of the courtiers spread first to the merchants, then to all burghers, and finally—of course in a modified form—to most of the people. Europeans imposed on themselves strategic planning, i.e., they no longer allow themselves to act on the spur of the moment, to follow impulses, but tend first to consider the consequences; their emotions are steadier, less erratic; they are cooler (Norbert Elias).

The external control became supplemented and partly supplanted by the "Super-Ego" (Freud). The western unconscious is guilt-ridden; individuals seek relief by confessing, by telling everything. Not so long ago you were expected to talk about sex (i.e., your sex problems); it was almost a must to participate in "consciousness-raising groups." The Maġribī on the other hand—still nearer to undifferentiated desire—"forgets" all the things one does not talk about.

MOROCCAN AND TOURIST

Since the Moroccan has a hard-on all the time, the tourist gets what he wants, but he should know that he just serves as an outlet for tension and frustration. He is just a hole, just a possibility of quick enjoyment—no reason to take care of him, since he is rich. Rašīd, a guy who hangs around the Café de France in al-Gueliz, the European quarter of Marrakeš, addressed me, his nostrils puffed up, his chest swollen out and accompanied by a Karate movement: "I'm Rašīd, called the ploughman of tourists. Can I help you?"

WHO IS THE RACIST?

Economic difficulties, social tensions, the war in the Sahara, Islāmistic agitation, tourism, and in particular the problems Moroccan workers and students face in France cause xenophobia to rise.

Last summer I witnessed how three guys attacked a French anthropologist and abused him as a "racist." Although it was long past midnight, I followed them to the lonely beach promenade, wanting to find out their motives.

I addressed the toughest one: "I must talk to you!" They were standing around the cart of a cigarette vendor, obviously drunk.

"All right," he replied. But the other two intervened angrily:

"*Zamel*," hissed one, "what do you want?"

"I'm on vacation."

"Whom are you passing your time with? Are you coming with me?" he wanted to know.

"Why?" I said, "are you a *zamel* as well?"

"Yes, we too," he screamed queenishly swishing his hips like a super-faggot. Then with his normal voice: "Do you buy me cigarettes?" (Note: We in the Third World are poor and need help, so do help!) and "Do you come home with me?"

"Why? Do you like men with a beard? And besides, you have money to buy alcohol, but not for cigarettes, how come?"

"You have a sharp tongue. You behave like a Moroccan although you are Italian. But we are Muslims. Is that clear?"

Not being able to fuck me (neither in the arse nor by words) they turned to another subject: The Muslim Holy War . . .

'My' man sent the others away; we talked about his hatred of the French . . .

Three men passed by: "*Salām ʿalaikum.* Where are you going to? Where are you going with this Christian?"

"*ʿAlaikum as-salām.* We were bored, so we decided to take a walk. I have nothing to do with him, he is but a *zamel.*" They left him alone. It was O.K. To be with a foreigner has to be justified to any Moroccan; when it is only a *zamel* it is all right; he is good for one thing and for one thing only: to get fucked. Everyone may use him.

When a foreigner is molested, is beaten up, nobody takes notice, nobody bothers. Just as, until their recent escape, the Jews served as the 'proper' outlet for aggression and hate, now the foreigners do. No reason for a Muslim to intervene. . . . But what a pleasure for a European homosexual to love somebody who robs, betrays, and fucks him at the same time.

THE HOMOSEXUAL DESIRE

Hegel (*Philosophie des Rechts*) and contemporary psychology see the beginning of humankind in the mastering of instincts. But what were these instincts, and how were they mastered? It is impossible to answer this question on the basis of one (one's own) society—being a prisoner of a net of inhibitions, restrictions and conditioning. Studying (and hopefully understanding) the sexual customs of a different society lets one's own assumptions appear in a new light and reveals their relativity. In all latitudes there is a primary mode of desire: a homosexual desire unconnected with the functioning of society, often secret, fleeting, and 'unconscious.' This desire is not yet the guilt-ridden fixed homosexuality formed by the Oedipal civilisation as defined by Guy Hocquenghem. The "passive" and "active" roles (*zamel* and *lūṭī* in the Arabo-Islāmic society) are not yet reified— as they become in all archaic-patriarchal societies.

There are many ways to integrate sexual impulses into society. There are many histories and many forms of social control trying to keep the balance between the demands of the collective and those of the individual. But in none of these histories is there room for pleasure and lust. Socially tamed, "socialized sexuality" is the only sexuality acceptable to society. Society forms, induces, expects certain forms of sexuality; it seeks to use the sexual needs of the individual to its advantage; it exploits sex in order to cut to size other forms of socialisation, other cultures are almost unknown.

A study of sexual customs in the Arabo-Islāmic world shows differences and similarities (both with our present situation and with our past). The most important difference lies in the absence of the dialectic of desire and prohibition (and hence of the dialectic of guilt and innocence, of offending of custom and anxiety for having offended them). Instead of all this one finds the dividing of sexuality into "pure" and "impure," i.e., into the poles of the Holy, and effective far reaching *external* controls instead of 'our' *internal* "super-ego." Such sexuality seems to be closer to an undifferentiated desire.

On the practical level there is room for something not found on the level of discourse (social speech): passion. The desire 'allows' the consciousness to open itself for one's own flesh and the flesh of the other. But the strong rejection of incarnation, a paranoid propensity to *negate* the act and annul the object, decodes *Islāmic* eroticism and reveals a refusal to accept a contamination of sex with emotion, love, or tenderness. The homosexual desire is reduced to the bare minimum, to a primitive state, half "nature," half "culture." Here the homosexual desire belongs not to the ego; it speaks of no place, it is inexpugnable, unconscious, invulnerable, irrevocable, and hence uncontrollable.

On the other hand the human 'carriers' of the desire are individuals and members of society, not merely arses and cocks functioning as unhistorical machines of desire. They are human beings having their own thoughts about happiness and togetherness.

We cannot live independent of society—innocently. We reproduce the economic, cultural, and emotional slavery of society by working, consuming, interacting, and having sex. Even desire and lust are not personal affairs only, even homosexual desire got formed by social institutions. Desire always presupposes the other, moves always toward the other before moving toward oneself, it tends to sociability and happiness—as yet unexplored continents. Maybe travelling the sexual and emotional lands of another culture helps to understand it—and to love better.

Moroccan Boys and Sex

Andreas Eppink
Jannie Figee (translator)

"The" Moroccan boy is brought up in a stern family with strict rules of pride, family honor, and consideration. At first there is for him nothing but the family, later boys of his quarter become important, and finally the world, i.e., the world of men.

At home sexuality is taboo (*harām*, holy, forbidden, protected). Bourdieu[1] and Demeerseman[2] say that discussing intimate matters would embarrass both parties, because they are seen as their respective personal 'insides.' Not hearing his parents discussing this subject, the boy has to get his sex education from the 'peer group.' So sexuality is seen as something not belonging to the family, something 'outside,' consequently suspect, shameful. The outside ('the street') is considered a source of bad influence, which could

---

In my study I tried as much as possible not to impose a theory on the data, neither to start from my frame of reference (European middle class sociological), nor from one found in the ethnological literature on the Arabs. Ordering the information I obtained in conversations with boys and girls from a medium sized Moroccan town—mainly middle class: clerks, small shopkeepers, craftsmen—I tried to see things in their (culture's) frame of reference, in their value system.

After elaborate discussions with a boy aged 22 and a girl aged 23 I wrote a questionnaire with 51 points for girls and 68 for boys, which were filled in by about twenty boys and twenty girls. The questions were in French and if necessary explained in Arabic by the two Moroccan interviewers.

Of special interest were the questions not fully understood by the respondents—thus revealing that these questions presupposed a European middle class frame of reference not applicable to Moroccans.

Most of my observations are confirmed by the French writer Duvert *Journal d'un innocent* (see note 13) and by studies among students of the American University of Beirut: Levon H. Melikian and E. Terry Prothro: *Sexual Behavior of University Students in the Arab Near East* in *The Journal of Abnormal and Social Psychology* 49, 1954 and Melikian: *Social Change and Sexual Behavior of Arab University Students* in *The Journal of Social Psychology* 73, 1967.

affect the family honor. The street and the danger of forbidden sex are also connected.

Here it has to be noted that particular acts are not so much judged according to an inner, 'absolute' standard as according to the situation in which the act takes place.[3] Sexuality itself is neither good nor bad: it depends on the situation.[4] There are, for example, situations that "make coition praiseworthy."[5] On the other hand, any coition outside marriage and concubinage is forbidden.

But there is less emphasis on what people do than on what becomes known. The stress is on 'good behavior' and 'consideration' (*liʿtibār*) not 'sin.'[6]

In order to regulate his sexual feelings and needs a Moroccan boy can either masturbate, accept passive anal contact (homosexual), or try to have active anal contact (homo-, heterosexual, or with animals) or heterosexual genital contact. Moroccans attach the highest value to the last, and the lowest to the first possibility mentioned. Never did the respondents mention oral-genital contact (kissing will be discussed later on).

SEX WITH FEMALES

In general the sexually mature boy will feel shame about approaching a girl or prostitute.[7] Because of the separation of the sexes and the seclusion of 'decent women,' any girl in the street is 'indecent,' is 'a whore.' The boy has little experience with girls of his age or unrelated women. He does not know how to behave in their presence. He feels a distance, if not fear.

Apart from family and fellow students a boy may only have contact with lower status women. Moreover every woman is considered to be unclean;[8] sexual intercourse with a woman during her period is forbidden.

On the one hand a boy running into a girl will want to have sex with her; he is expected to show his virility by instant sex with any woman on her own; but on the other hand he will be afraid—certainly the first time.

In North Africa everyone is taught to do things with others: a child is not encouraged to do things on its own or to develop self reliance. In the peer group one feels safe and strong.

A boy scarcely dares to do something of which he is not sure that his friends approve. It hardly happens that a boy 'sees' a girl alone. Normally the most courageous one tries to pick up a 'prostitute' with whom they all have intercourse one by one. When everything is shared, so are the girls; what is good for my friends is good for me, and vice versa. (But this changes after marriage when sexual intercourse will be an exclusive prerogative of the husband.)

What a Westerner might take as lack of privacy is seen by Moroccans as security: as long as one sees that others do the same as you do, there is no need to be afraid or to feel shame.

MASTURBATION

Masturbation as a possibility for sexual fulfilment is strongly repudiated and least valued, because it lacks an object.[9] This has to do with the value attached to intromission and ejaculation.[10] [11]

In the Western middle-class frame of reference, sexuality is highly related to eroticism and love. This is by no means the case in all cultures and in all times. Vanggaard describes types of aggressive sexuality in cultures of pre-Christian Europe: The sexual act of the active man is intended to make the object passive, to submit him.[12] This seems to be true for North Africa as well. Masturbating—not submitting some other person—is not manly; therefore '*kaffat*/masturbator' is a term of abuse.

Nevertheless (fitting the pattern of group security) boys often masturbate together, outside, or in a room, or at the movies where it is quite common. This is done touching each other, but it is not normal to look at each other's penis and to talk about it.

Masturbation is one of the most delicate topics to talk about. Often it is claimed that it is not necessary, "because there are so many other possibilities."

MALE-MALE SEX

In fact it is more likely that in a country where women tend to be segregated, masturbation is necessary because there are not so many other possibilities . . . unless one gets up the courage to do it with younger boys. Peers and friends are your equals and therefore difficult to submit; and women are kept away from you; and if you were to chance upon a girl, the lack of experience in contact with them remains a great hindrance.

With younger boys these barriers do not exist: they are younger, therefore they can be submitted; going with them does not cause shame. Therefore boys look for younger boys (7-13 years old) who are 'fit' for this.[13] Persuasion is effected by nice words, money or force. From my conversations it is clear that tips are exchanged about boys/young men/men who could be/are 'fit.' Usually one cannot claim somebody for oneself. A 'personal' relation between an 'active' and a 'passive' boy is exceptional, not to mention a love relation. (Anyhow that is the opinion stated by the interviewees.) But it may happen that one feels a strong sexual attraction toward a particular boy.

This 'informing' has as a consequence that some boys get the reputation of *zāmel* (somebody submitting to anal intercourse). If a boy has this image it will be most difficult for him to submit another from his own circle; he will be forced to fulfil the passive role until he goes outside his circle or gets married.

The striking aspect of this pattern is the distinction between 'active' and 'passive,'[14] thus creating two categories: men (in hetero- or homosexual intercourse) and non-men—males known to be both agens and patiens being exceedingly rare.

SEX—AFFECTION—LOVE

As we already saw the emphasis in sexual contacts between boys is not on friendship or romantic love, but on penetration and ejaculation. This is true for relations between male and female as well. Friendship, being possible only between equals, can exist between men of the same status/age group and between women of equal status. The relation with a sexual object—boy, woman or 'buggered one'—is a relation with an inferior; penetration is felt to be a manifestation of male power. Sex is, essentially penetration.[15]

A boy told me: "We are so quickly excited and therefore we want the 'act' at once, otherwise we would lose our semen early." No emphasis is given to sexual excitement by caressing, foreplay and petting. A 'real man' prefers intromission and quick ejaculation.

This does not mean that affection is never felt; but romantic love does not predominate in a sexual relationship (nor in marriage).

Kissing[16] and oral-genital contact are not customary. Foreplay and petting—like masturbation—are held to be inferior; such behavior is often labelled as 'weak' or 'strange.'

MARRIED MEN—CELIBATES

Marriage both offers the possibility of lawful, unproblematic intromission and confirms the status of adult man (women's status only improves with the birth of the first boy). Without marriage one is not 'a real man,' not a full member of society.

Some married men will continue to have anal intercourse with boys or their wives or both. This was repeatedly indicated in conversations, but contradicted by others. Some said that while the man might like to have anal intercourse with his wife, she would repudiate this, as boys were the more suitable object for it. Premarital sex, however, could often be anal in order to preserve the girl's virginity.[17]

For whatever reason, quite a number of married men go on looking for (young) boys.[18] This is all right provided the man does not neglect his wife sexually.

Somebody old enough to and capable of supporting a wife, yet who does not marry, is abused as *zūfri* (celibate). When he is still looking for boys, it is called childlike. Here it is interesting to note that a distinction is made: to wit, whether somebody is having intercourse with boys as well, or exclusively. The first can boast of his exploits; he is sometimes admiringly called *howāi* (big fuck) or *saḥšāḥ* (good seducer). The latter is regarded with scorn.

Even worse is the man who lets others use him as patiens; he is called 'no-real-man' or '*ḥassās*'. The penetratee is strongly condemned and scorned.

CONCLUSION

In the Moroccan cultural pattern genital (heterosexual) penetration is the most highly valued form of sexuality, since it is considered to be the most active. But for youth, sex with other boys is a more likely sexual outlet and is accepted as an initial experience. The attitude toward the 'active' is positive, toward the 'passive' boy one of tolerant pity, and toward the adult who gets penetrated, one of scorn. Alternating between penetrating and being penetrated is rare. The only escape for a patiens is marriage.

In Morocco—as among working class Americans of the Fifties[19] —sexuality is seen as neutral in itself, but it has to be regulated, ideally in marriage. If sex is not confined therein, people can excuse it by saying that man is weak and Allāh forgiving. But not only is the frame important; so is the form: active/on top/above/*fauq*/male, or passive/laid/at the bottom/below/*taḥt*/female.

Comparing our results with Kinsey's data (North America 1949) we found many points in common with his 'lower level,' such as:

- taking intromission as the essential activity in 'normal' sexual behavior (Kinsey p. 369),
- rejection of masturbation (Kinsey p. 375) and petting, kissing (Kinsey p. 369),
- acceptance of hetero- and homosexual sex from childhood (Kinsey p. 383),
- no conflicting loyalties with regard to hetero- and homosexual activities during the same period (Kinsey p. 361),
- acceptance of the 'active' role in homosexual anal contact (Kinsey p. 616) and sometimes continuation of these contacts, even after marriage (Kinsey p. 384).

In Morocco the main distinction is not between hetero- and homosexuality (i.e., the choice of the sex of the partner), but between 'activity' and 'passivity' (penetration), i.e., the choice of the form of sexual behavior, regardless of the sex of the partner. Friendship, romantic love, and sexual intercourse are thought of as distinct and hardly 'combinable.'

NOTES

1. P. Bourdieu: *The Sentiment of Honour in Kabyle Society* in *Honour and Shame* (ed. J.G. Peristany), London, 1965.

2. A. Demeerseman: *La famille Tunisienne et les temps nouveaux*, Tunis, 1972.

3. L. Gardet: *L'Islam*, 1959, and P. Shustery: *Outlines of Islamic Culture*, Gagalore, 1954.

4. Charnay: *Pluralisme normatif et ambiguité dans le Fiqh*, Paris, 1967, p. 183: « . . . l'acte sexuel . . . est (si les interdictions légales sont respectées) neutre en lui même».

5. Charnay, 1967: «peuvent rendre louable l'acte sexuel».

6. Charnay, 1967.

7. Prostitution is common in towns; the prices are low so that even young boys can afford them.

8. Cf. E. Westermarck: *Ritual and Belief in Morocco*, London, 1928, vol. II p. 3; uncleanness is seen "as loaded with magic influence" and therefore one tries to have to do with it as little as possible.

9. Kinsey, 1949, p. 375: "At lower levels, and particularly among the older generations of the lowest level, masturbation may be looked down upon as abnormal, a perversion, an infantile substitute for socio-sexual contacts."

10. Since all of my informants have attended primary school during the French protectorate, and thus mastered French, the discussions were held in that language; they spoke of "the act/l'acte."

11. Kinsey, 1949, p. 369: "Many persons at the lower level consider that intromission is the essential activity and the only justifiable activity in a 'normal' sexual relation."

12. Vanggaard; *Phallos*, 1971, p. 95: ,, . . . daß gewisse Beziehungen, die für uns lediglich eine sexuelle Bedeutung haben, von den Alten im Lichte der Herrschaft oder Unterwerfung gesehen wurden, d.h. in der Sphäre der Aggression fielen.“ (certain relation being for us only sexual were seen by the Anciens in the light of dominance or submission) and p. 103/4: ,,Ich habe betont, daß die Männer . . . vom Verlangen nach einem gewaltsamen analen Koitus erfüllt waren, dem als treibende Kraft Aggression und nicht Erotik zugrunde lag. Das soll natürlich nicht besagen, daß mit dem Orgasmus, der sich aus solchem gewaltsamen Tun ergibt, kein Lustempfinden verbunden ist. Aber zunächst hat ein solcher Akt nicht mit erotischen Gefühlen zu tun. Er ist nicht der Ausdruck

warmer Zuneigung, des Verlangens nach Vereinigung sowie eines Wunsches, zu geben und zu nehmen, zu besitzen und sich besitzen zu lassen. Vielmehr handelt es sich hier in erster Linie um eine Befreiung von aggressiver Spannung, eine Äuβerung des Verlangens, Macht auszuüben, zu unterwerfen, zu demütigen und dem Opfer die Manneskraft zu nehmen.“ (I stressed that men were driven by an aggressive—not erotic—desire for anal coition. That is not to say that orgasm resulting from rape is without lust. Yet primarily it is not an expression of warm affection, of an erotic desire for union, of the wish to give and to take, to possess and to be possessed. It is rather release of aggressive tension, an expression of the desire to dominate, to subjugate, to humilitate and to rob the victim of his virility.)

13. Duvert; *Journal d'un innocent*, Paris, 1976, p. 77: «Je ne crois évidemment pas le chiffre, mais la chose est banale: un cul percé attire les jeunes célibataires de la populace comme un pot de miel fait venir les mouches. On se nomme le coupable, on en parle, on va à lui quand on a besoin à soulager, et quelquefois on le contraint: ce serait révoltant qu'il refuse, puisqu'il est déjà troué.» (. . . from the moment an arse-hole is pierced it attracts the bachelors like a pot of honey attracts the bees. One gives the name of the fallen one to the other, one speaks about it, one goes to him whenever the need arises. Sometimes he is raped; it is out of the question for him to refuse once the entrance is made.) p. 78: «un garçon sera l'homosexuel [le pénétré] du groupe parce qu'il a regardé, désiré, sollicité avant qu'un autre s'y décide. On ne voit pas le désir (on est en train d'apprendre à le chasser), on repère le trou et on l'utilise. Un enfant obéissant se ferme l'anus: celui qui garde le sien ouvert devient le putain des autres garçons et donc les aide à sauver leur propre trou. C'est comme un jeu éducatif: on serre les fesses ensemble, le premier qui relâche est pédé.» (one boy will be fucked by the rest of the group, because he gazed, he seemed to desire it, to beg for it more than anybody else. The desire of the fucker is ignored, he just fills a hole, uses an arse. A good boy keeps his arse tight. The one, who does not seal it, becomes the whore of the other boys, thus helping them to keep theirs intact. . . .)

14. Some speak of 'positive' and negative.'

15. C. von Balen (*Erotik des Ostens*, 1955) remarks that ejaculation is the centre of Arab eroticism (p. 160). The concentration on vaginal and anal intromission can become understandable. An informer told me: «Pour se satisfaire, on peut prendre tout: la femme, l'âne ou la vache.» (“To satisfy oneself one can take everything: woman, donkey or cow.”)

16. Duvert, op. cit. p. 163: «Puis j'ai appris que le baiser à la français était peu répandu dans les flirts: on bisote, on picore le visage, on se prend pas les langues. Les baisers vus au cinéma n'y changent rien.» (I noticed that French kisses are quite uncommon in spite of what is shown in the pictures.) Kinsey, op. cit. p. 369: “Many a college male will have kissed dozens of girls, although he has had intercourse with none of them. On the other hand, the lower level male is likely to have had intercourse with hundreds of girls, but he may have kissed a few of them . . . for he is likely to have considerable distaste for the deep kiss which is fairly common in upper level histories.”

17. The concept 'virginity' is a question of shame—not of 'guilt.' A man takes possesion of a wife and does not want a second-hand item; the father wants to give his daughter intact to her husband, otherwise she is 'worth' nothing. The virginal membrane is proof of her value, as it shows that she was well guarded and is 'virtuous.'

18. Kinsey, op.cit. p. 384: ". . . it is not surprising to find a fair number of the males at (the lower) level continuing both types of activity through the major portion of their lives. It is notable, however, that there are few individuals in this group who become exclusively homosexual. There are some who definitely condemn the homosexual, but there are many who accept it simply as one more form of sex." Ibid. p. 631.: "(In very remote rural areas) homosexual activity rarely conflicts with heterosexual relations, and is quite without the argot, physical manifestations, and other affections so often found in urban groups. There is a minimum of personal disturbance or social conflict over such activity."

19. Kinsey, op. cit. p. 383: "At the lowest level, sex, whether it be heterosexual or homosexual, is more or less accepted as inevitable. The children here are the least restrained sexually and usually become involved in both heterosexual and homosexual activities at an early age."

Among Syrian Men

Gary B. MacDonald

Say hello to Zuzu, the most famous faggot in one of the world's oldest cities. He is an attractive middle-aged man who drinks too much. Dressed in a scarf, billowing shirt unbuttoned to the navel, and tight pants, Zuzu takes to the streets at night in search of the willing men he knows are there. He hangs out in the fashionable Abu Rumaneh quarter of Damascus, where the more Westernized, wealthier men are less likely to beat him up. There, he cruises sidewalk cafes and shouts imprecations to passing cars in a slurred bleat of a voice. Cars full of teen-aged boys pull up. The exhilaration of the hunt, and condescension of conquest, are evident in Zuzu's heightened theatricality and the car occupants' shrill laughter. But the cars move on. Zuzu spies a passerby. Mincing across four lanes of traffic, he shakes the man's hand and instinctively gropes him. The man looks embarrassed but does not resist. Another car full of men comes along, the two of them get in. Zuzu has connected.

The man called Zuzu is the lone exposed tip of Syria's gay iceberg. He is afloat in very deep waters indeed. His public flaunting of common but carefully hidden behavior is as close to a political statement as Syrian gays get. Men, including gay men, despise and ridicule this pioneer, perhaps never more vehemently than when they are using him. They also respect him. Zuzu's bravery is a grand gesture Syrians cannot help but admire. His camp and costume are refractions of the femininity latent in all men (and in Syria, where men are unusually soft, open effeminacy cuts close to the bone). But what really dumbfounds Syrians is Zuzu's gleeful passivity. In a society where only men fuck and only women get fucked, he is a man who gets fucked *and likes it*. This unthinkable confession of abnormality makes Zuzu a modern-day shaman. He acts out, thus exorcises, the sexual ambiguities inherent in the condition of being a Syrian man.

Like all men in Syria, Zuzu was born into a society in which birth is still destiny, and one's sex at birth even more so. Conventional wisdom holds that a man, just by virtue of being male, is stronger, calmer, bolder, wiser, smarter—in short, just plain better—than a woman. This conviction defines the family, which remains Syria's stongest institution despite (or perhaps because of) the ravages of rapid modernization. It is in the family that the primordial responsibility of the "bearer of seed" is first exaggerated out of all proportion. The male alone is active; he *gives*. The female alone is passive; she *receives*. The possession of a penis or a vagina is a tautology.

Growing up male in Syria is full of contradictions. On the one hand, it entails marvelous perks that lead the boy into thinking that the world is his oyster. The Syrian boychild is coddled and stroked, humored, and even fed more than his sisters. He is constantly the centre of attention, and learns to take centrestage for granted. There, the earnest little actor is drilled by everyone from parents to corner vegetable merchant in the litanies and rituals of manhood. By the time he enters school, his instruction in gender privilege has made him a willing initiate in the mystical fraternity of his sex. And in the Syrian schools, the separation of boys and girls only encourages the male-bonding for which groundwork has been laid down in the home.

On the other hand, the boy quickly discovers that gender privilege is no defense against the wider world for which he is being prepared. Syria is a police state in which whatever consensus exists is achieved through a gun barrel. Damascus itself looks and feels like an armed camp. Life is expensive, inefficient, and quixotically violent. Constant political turmoil requires a standing army in which young men are obligated to serve (and in whose ranks they frequently die). Opportunities for upward mobility are so limited as to be virtually non-existent. Except in engineering or medicine, even a university degree guarantees no more than a life of menial office labor or worse.

In short, the freedom of privilege for which a man's youth supposedly destined him turns out to have a flip side. He grew up expecting to live a leitmotif from Rossini, when in fact the conditions of his life are more nearly Wagnerian.

In this tightly controlled social context, where loneliness and ennui are common symptoms of the malaise, Zuzu is bound to make a mockery of "the way things are." He defies the unnatural insularity of Syrian mores by reminding his peers that human nature is by definition richly complex. His antics also subvert the notion that Syrian men are always in charge; always, so to speak, on top. "Oh yeah?" Zuzu's sly wink insinuates. "Prove it!"

But Zuzu drinks, as many do, because he is so terribly alone. His gay brothers (and sisters) are in hiding, barricaded behind a wall of secrecy that would withstand a nuclear blast. Fear of disclosure is profound, and necessary, in a state that punishes homosexual acts with death (statute is said to be rarely enforced, although one hears stories to the contrary). But even the death penalty is less feared than disclosure before one's family and friends. Gays tremble merely to imagine the ostracism that would result from this most important act of coming out. Compared to it, self-imposed exile is trivial.

People carrying on in private, however, rarely meet others doing the same. Syrian gays do not know one another. There are no exclusively gay bars, discos, or restaurants, nor even establishments where gays are known to congregate. There are, rather, little gay cells composed of five to ten individuals, usually lifelong friends. They see each other daily or from time to time as a group in a member's home. One cell may occasionally encounter another, or one of its members may have an affair with the member of another cell, and so, slowly and cautiously, the gay social organism grows. But it always grows by chance, never deliberately. Even when new lines of communication are established, little effort goes into maintaining them. That would be dangerous because any kind of grouping increases the risk of exposure. Thus, something like the following is a constant lament: "Whatever happened to those boys down in Kasaā (the Christian quarter of Damascus)? I heard they moved to Beirut, but I don't know. I never see them anymore."

Alone, lonely, and perpetually on the prowl, the Syrian gay casts himself adrift in his natural habitat: the street. There he finds a veritable ocean of dark, lithe, well-hung men. Any night of the week they can be found in profusion, crowding lane and boulevard to take the evening air. Among them, gays search for the one, true lover of their lives. But if Mr. Right cannot be found, there are hundreds of Mr. *Mašihāl* (not so bad) whose bodies assuage the disappointment.

Syrian men are very available. The meaning of the word "straight" has been bent in practice to mean: he always likes women but he often prefers men.

Consider the traffic in taxi drivers, for example. Gay friends of mine invest in expensive cab rides the way others sink money into bonds. The return is excellent, and usually guaranteed. Conversations between chauffeur and gay passenger quickly establish the former's matrimonial status. If he is single, he is shamelessly asked, "Well, then, who yanks it for you." "Just me." Laughter all around. "That's a shame. It's better to have company." "Yes, but, you know, company is hard to find." "No, it's not. I'll do it for you." More often than not the driver agrees. A friend, ill with a high fever, was once being sped to a hospital when he noticed that his driver was cute. Physician and malady were quickly forgotten, they adjourned to my friend's apartment and made literally feverish love. "He was the best I ever had," grinned the patient, who recovered, "but I never saw him again." Another time, a different driver and fare were caught *in flagrante delicto* on the outskirts of Damascus. Rather than turn them in, however, the two young policemen turned them over and exacted their own, more satisfying punishment. One of its victims later confided, "It was heaven. That cop was this long."

Taxi lore is a colorful mainstay of gay gossip. Other varieties of anonymous sex are more pedestrian. The usual pair or trio of gays afoot and at work is easily distracted, and has developed its own language to compare distractions. Chattering away in Arabic, they will suddenly spy a "scene" (handsome man) who noticeably possesses a "true" (large cock) and indisputably is someone "TDF" (To Die For). On the other hand, if during discussions a "shabo" (untrustworthy person, possibly secret police) should intervene, then it is advisable to "wa-wa" (change the subject). No one within earshot understands a word, not even other gays, who may have their own vocabularies.

Street cruising action is all in the eyes, and since Syrians have no qualms about direct eye contact, it is all the more thrilling to test the difference between an invitation and an ordinary stare. The hunt is made even more ambiguous by the lack of fashion markers of gay identity now prevalent in the West; in Damascus, everyone dresses, looks, and acts pretty much the same. So a come-on, when detected, can be scandalously long, limpid, and languorous; eyes look for whole minutes and never even stray to the crotch. Once contracted, however, liaisons are rarely consummated in public. There are interesting stories to the contrary, like the one about an Eastern diplomat who used to go into a stall in a public toilet (called "embassies" by gays), lower his trousers, bend over and lose count of how many times he would be fucked—often with surprising finesse, considering the surroundings—before he simply got tired and had to sit down. But for the most part, innate Arab modesty dictates a more private quickie at home, at someone else's home, or in one of a few safe, semi-public places such as a Turkish bath, or *ḥammām*.

It was in just such a steamy locale that months of frustrated searching led me (by chance, of course) to meet my first Syrian gays. There were three of them relaxing in towels after a bath, and they were carrying on in a manner that could only mean one thing. Figuring I had everything to gain, I sat next to them and demanded indelicately, "Are you gay?"

"Of course, honey," one of them, Adnan, replied. Thereupon the adventure began.

(All names have been changed. Syrians employed in the oppression of their own people who read this article looking for clues will be pleased to know that the names I have used throughout in no instance match those of any of my Syrian friends, gay or straight.)

Adnan quickly became a friend. Though in many ways atypical of his gay peers, he provided strong first hints of what to expect. He was 23, unemployed, and living at home with his parents and three younger brothers (one of whom was also gay). He had not finished high school because his father wanted him to work in the family business, but he disliked that business and was waiting for an uncle to arrange a job for him in Saudi Arabia ("where the boys are"). He had learned his good, idiomatic English by listening to the BBC and disco music. Adnan shared with most gays a weakness for foreigners, and spent a lot of time at a luxury hotel with Lufthansa stewards when they were in town. Otherwise he tricked often, and "my gay friends and I have had sex I don't know how many times."

Adnan also had a lover—Fayez, an army officer—with whom he was conducting an affair complicated by the fact that Fayez resisted admitting he was gay. This was hardly unusual, but Fayez was hard to peg. In behavior, attitudes, and affections, he was neither heterosexual nor homosexual exclusively, nor even what is called bisexual. He roamed all over Kinsey's scale, stumbling into sexual encounters when and if they presented themselves. The sex or preference of a particular partner mattered as little to him as the color of his socks (which were often mismatched). Yet he was both homophobic and a misogynist! In the end, it was hard to tell what Fayez liked, or if he really liked anything at all. He was typical of a whole new class of young people, who might be called the urban lost, that is being created now in developing countries: clever in superficial ways calculated to appear "Western," a gifted mimic of behaviors not his own, ambitious and thoroughly amoral, a user; the sort of person for whom Syrians have coined the term "empty vessel."

Naturally, this gave much grief to Adnan. "He is so dull in bed," Adnan complained. "He'll kiss me or touch me sometimes, but I always have the feeling that he doesn't want to. So he lies there while I make love to him, and then he fucks me. He won't even say he likes that, but I know he does. He cries often when he comes."

My sympathy for Adnan's predicament grew more and more guarded, however, when we became boyfriends. The ironies were stunning. He enjoyed my testing the *Joy of Gay Sex* repertoire on his willing body (with one exception: he would not let me fuck him). *His* routine consisted solely of a few tight-lipped pecks before he got down to the chore of jerking me off. This he did with all the warmth of a milking machine. When he discovered he could fuck me, even kissing (such as it was) fell by the wayside. Thereafter his conduct between the sheets amounted to an artless, urgent campaign whose only object was climax. In response to my eventual suggestion that he was treating me as badly as Fayez treated him, Adnan listened politely, then in a small voice replied, "You're not the first one to tell me the same thing." Apparently his Lufthansa buddies had been thinking along similar lines. I though I had made my point, but no; immediately after our heart-to-heart, Adnan flipped me over and . . . it was the end of our affair.

Not all Syrian gays are as insensitive as Adnan, but most are as conscious of the role they play in bed. Masculine/active, feminine/passive are separate sides of the bed, and few possess the passport of self-acceptance that permits free passage back and forth. Men are not "real" men if they behave passively in sex, and illusion driven home relentlessly by a culture that insists that, in practice, anyway, gay men are women. In short, they exist to be exploited. This keenly felt (and of course irrevocable) deficiency is the essence of gay self-loathing and a self-replenishing source of frustration. It explains why Adnan eagerly played the "man" with me, while with others he meekly became the "woman." Or, as a friend once put it, "When I find a man who will let me fuck *him*, I become crazy. There are so few who do anything but fuck *me*."

Male socialization produces an anomaly at the heart of Syrian sexual dynamics, gay or straight. While all men are expected to relate sexually only to women, most have been brought up to relate emotionally only to other men. As a result, both heterosexual and homosexual relationships are rarely sensitive, reciprocal acts of respect and affection. Men find it hard to link sex and emotion in liaisons with women, and almost impossible to do so in peccadillos involving other men. Outside the bedroom, relationships are conceptualized sentimentally; sunsets or storms are always forming on the horizon as the violins sing. But in bed, where instinct strips sentiment, men tend to be emotionless and mechanical. Like Latins in the famous line, Syrians are lousy lovers.

In addition, a curious homosexualization of male social relations occurs, the manifestations of which are as deceptive as they are obvious. Syrian men are intensely sensual creatures who touch themselves and each other constantly. One sees them everywhere, walking arm in arm or holding hands and kissing. They are also gentler and more maternal with each other than is common among males elsewhere. There is a softness at the core of male relationships that would be charming (and very sexy) were it not so ineffectual. The softness masks, and in part compensates, the most debilitating effect of a Syrian man's upbringing: his difficulty in relating sexually *and* emotionally to the same human being.

This debility has particularly melancholic consequences for gays. They must puzzle out the connection between their own emotions and sexuality, and *deal* with similar confusion in their sexual partners. It is a no-win situation that quickly wears people down. Gays react with resignation and promiscuity, seeking literally to fuck the blues away. In practice this obscures the ways in which, as men, Syrian gays continue to exploit the masculine privilege (over other men instead of women) that is their birthright.

A case in point was an evening I spent at the apartment of an acquaintance named Abdulaziz, chatting with him and a friend, Ali. At some point Hussein, who was 16, and his cousin, Majed, dropped by. Majed was visiting from Homs; he was 18, dark, shy, and willowy. They could only stay for a moment because Hussein's parents were waiting for them at home. The moment stretched to three hours, during which Majed dazzled us all. Small wonder: he was gorgeous.

When Hussein and Majed got up to go at 11:30 Abdulaziz suggested they stay longer. They hesitated long enough for Ali to snatch Majed into the bedroom. The rest of us, with studied *sang-froid*, sat down again, and acted as if nothing had happened. Five minutes later, Ali called for Abdulaziz from the bedroom. Abdulaziz went to the door, and on my way to the bathroom I passed him peeking. When I came back, Ali was sitting on the sofa with Hussein, looking flushed and moody. Abdulaziz had disappeared.

Soon, Ali moved next to me across the room and launched into a (for him) unusual soliloquy. "Majed wanted me, but I didn't think I'd like him and I didn't. He's not my type, you know? [I did; Ali was exclusively passive.] So I thought I'd start him, and Abdulaziz could finish him." Ali stared at the floor for a moment. "I hate the men I go to bed with. They fuck me once, and I never want to see them again. So I look for love first, before sex, because if I love him he can fuck me more than once." Ali laughed ruefully. "I don't have much luck.

"And," he concluded, "I *never* go to bed with gay friends, not even with Abdulaziz. I would hate them, too, like all the others."

Now Abdulaziz called for tissues from the bedroom. Hussein jumped up to get them. As he disappeared, Ali gazed at me meaningfully and, with perfect comic timing, said, "Gay life is very interesting." We could not help laughing.

Abdulaziz appeared shortly in his bikini briefs and made straight for Ali. "What's the matter? Didn't you like him?" Ali demurred. "He's very easy," Abdulaziz said with an impish grin.

Then Majed appeared, looking no one in the eye, and almost ran to the bathroom to wash. He left the door open, though, and through it he must have heard Abdulaziz and Ali discussing his endowment in detail. They were like two eager buyers comparing a used car. When Majed re-emerged finally, I noticed a magnificent hickey blooming on his neck. I pulled his sweater collar up to cover it, and he smiled lamely in thanks. Abdulaziz and Ali instantly began to argue about who was responsible for the hickey. Not once did they address or even acknowledge Majed, who stood nearby shifting uneasily from foot to foot. In fact, when Hussein and Majed had gone a few minutes later, I realized that none of us had even said goodbye.

Such indifference to the feelings of one's own is by no means unique to Syrian gay males. But the isolation and furtiveness that promote it do mean that there are few options to behave otherwise. It is sobering to consider just how grim the prospects really are for gays in a country such as Syria. None of the conditions presently exist there that in the West have led from industrialization to affluence to social pluralism to feminism to, finally, the gay liberation movement. Only in this century have Western gays begun to focus on the quality of homosexual life, and only in the last decade have we actively begun to do something about it. It would be arrogant to accuse our Syrian brothers of being any more "backward" than we still are. They are simply far less lucky. The tragedy of their lives, indeed of the region in which they live, seemingly has no end.

So it is remarkable how sensitive, warm, and generous the Syrians have remained, despite the formidable odds against them. They party seriously, as only people who understand the profound value of good times and laughter can.

I remember one party in particular. We were eight people gathered at Abdulaziz's apartment. Adnan was there. So were two middle-aged men, both married, one as prim as the other was bohemian (the latter, Abdulaziz noted, kept apartments all over town and provided keys to friends for tricking), and two younger men, one of whom was tall and voluptuous while his companion looked like a refugee from a Polo boutique.

The party began, as all such affairs did, with a review of snapshots of the last party. These were passed from hand to hand with the syncopation of a ladies' high tea complete with sighs and swooning, and then were put away. Abrupt change of tone: someone switched on the ubiquitous Eurodisco tape and people began dancing. Voluptuous and Clone sucked each other off in a dark corner. Adnan and I caught up on gossip with Prim. Suddenly, the music stopped and the lights went out. Another power outage? No, it was time for "Camellia."

Protruding from a side door was a slender, shapely leg clad in one of those delicate sandals that immortalize the ankle but ruin the instep. At the other end of the leg came Abdulaziz, unfolding into the room like a silk scarf, dressed in a pert straw hat, camisole, and skirt. Except for the moustache and hairy chest, he might have stepped out of the pages of *Vogue*. Accompanied by a driving disco beat, Camellia performed a precisely choreographed dance, acknowledged her whistles and applause, and retired to the wings.

Immediately, everyone rushed for the bathroom to change. Plastic shopping bags full of provisions were produced from nowhere, and the air grew thick with perfume as people exchanged wigs, scarves, mascara and lipstick, skirts, stockings, and shoes. Some of the men had brought three changes of clothing; one had sewn everything he wore. The cassette was changed to oriental music and, one after another, all of the ladies present got up and belly-danced.

Nothing in my years in the Middle East was more fascinating than the accomplished allure of my companions as they danced. In a country where competition determined female charms, my friends put to shame the best women belly-dancers, and they knew it. The comfort this gave them was affecting. Encouraged by the music's atonal whump and twang, they twirled and ground their hips in an intricate paean to sex that, for a moment at least, permitted them to forget the ironies of their own sexuality.

The dancing told a story that was at once alienated, humorous, sly, self-deprecating, celebratory, fearful, sensual, and sad.

It was also Zuzu's story. At that very moment, he was probably weaving along the boulevards, engaged in another kind of play. His nocturnal sojourns, like the sinuous bodies behind closed doors, are what being born to lose in Syria is all about.

EDITOR'S COMMENT

Gary MacDonald's article, published in 1984 in *The Body Politic*, a Canadian newspaper no longer in publication and not held by many libraries, gives a lively account of the scene in Damascus. For these reasons we wanted to include it in this reader, although we respectfully disagree with the paragraphs mentioning Zuzu (i.e., paragraphs 1, 2, 3, 7, 8, and the last).

Unlike MacDonald, I think the Syrian macho does not see himself as *giving*, but rather as *taking* (what he wants); it is the fuckee who gives—his body, his ass. The opposition I came across in Syria was "doing" and "being done." In his statement "the possession of a penis and a vagina is the tautology" I believe MacDonald wants to say "that men fuck and women get fucked goes without saying."

Jehoeda Sofer points out in the article "Sodomy in the Law of Muslim States" that the Syrian Penal Code does not prescribe the death penalty for sodomy—contrary to MacDonald's statement in paragraph 8.

Furthermore, we hope by now it is clear to all our readers that the term *gay* is not consonant to the oriental concepts of sexuality among males and does not do justice to their reality. The "Preface" and the articles "Different Approaches to Male-Male Sexuality/ Eroticism from Morocco to Usbekistān," "An Italian in Morocco," "Transvestites and Transsexuals in Turkey," and "Arab Men in Paris" explain this concept.

Concerning two of MacDonald's observations I want to propose a different interpretation:

1. He believes fear to be the main reason for maintaining only *small* social circles. I, on the other hand, believe the reason to be disinterest: the "girls" (Syrian Arabic *manyakin*—fuckees) give each other social and *emotional* support, for sex they prefer "real" men.

2. MacDonald holds "innate Arab modesty" responsible for the preference of "more private quickies" over "tearoom" sex. The fact that the "Eastern diplomat" had no problems in finding uncountable Syrians willing to fuck him in public, demonstrates to me that the explanation lies not in innate modesty of the fucker but rather in the reluctance of the fuckee to make his "dishonor" too apparent.

Arno Schmitt

AUTHOR'S REPLY

As to your question regarding the meaning of my statement, "The possession of a penis and a vagina is a tautology," which occurs at the end of the third paragraph of my essay, I meant to summarize the paragraph that it concludes. I used the word tautology in a looser sense of its meaning in logic, i.e., "a statement that is true because it provides for all logical possibilities." In the third paragraph I tried to convey the point that, in the Syrian cultural mind as I understand it, gender defines behavior. A Syrian male does certain things and does not do others because he is a male. In terms of the rigid code of Syrian male sexuality, therefore, a male fucks but does not get fucked. He fucks because he has a penis and a penis is designed only for fucking (or, as I put it, giving). A Syrian female gets fucked because she has a vagina and a vagina is designed only for being fucked (or receiving). By extension, a male cannot get fucked because he is not a female. In this cultural logic, the possession of a penis is in fact a tautology because, for Syrians, the only logical possibility is that penises fuck.

Gary B. MacDonald

Intimate Look of the Iranian Male

Jerry Zarit

What, I often thought during the four years I lived in Tehran, would all those Iranians do without us foreigners?

Now, with the Shah out and the Ayatollah in, I wonder about that more than ever.

Looking back to the vanished prerevolutionary Iran I knew and loved and hated, I can see in retrospect that the mutually dependent, complex relations between gay foreigner and Iranian male were part of a much larger collision between East and West.

Iran was for me, and for others like me, a sexual paradise. In terms of both quantity and quality it was the most exciting experience of my life.

Yet with one or two possible exceptions, I never met an Iranian in his own country who would completely acknowledge his homosexuality.

Cultural concepts differ from one society to another, and sexual behavior in Iran, like any other form of behavior, was the result of cultural conditioning that in ways was very different from our own.

Sex roles, attitudes toward them, and even the language expressing them was different. Almost all men I had sex with would more accurately be called bisexual than gay. Yet even that term does not adequately account for the much greater degree to which those males made themselves available than their Western counterparts, or the startling openness and aggressiveness with which they often made known their intentions. To compare them to Western-style hustlers might bring one somewhat closer to the truth, for, while money was by no means always part of the game, both the hustler and the Iranian have the notion that their masculinity and heterosexuality are not affected by sexual relations with other males.

You may have guessed by now, if you did not already know, what these 'straight' Iranians most often liked to do in bed (and in alleys, parks, theaters, moving and parked vehicles, construction sites, etc.): They were trade, i.e., they took the masculine role both anally and orally, fucking being by far the preferred activity. *Kuni*, one of the Farsi words for 'queer' reveals the importance of this role. A *kuni* is somebody who gives his ass (*kun*). Words reflect attitudes, and thus by definition the fucker is in no danger of being considered queer. The fuckee usually did it in secret or rationalized it by demanding money for his services, or was a foreigner like me.

The Iranian preoccupation with anal sex amounted to an obsession. Jokes and insults abounded, and the expressed desire of one male to get into his friend's pants was frequently taken as a good-natured jest. Farsi has two complementary words for 'pimp,' one meaning a procurer of vagina (*koskeš*) and the other of ass (*kunkeš*).

Young boys were especially in demand. The scene in Michener's *Caravans* in which one man murders another in a fight over the favors of a dancing-boy is not too far away from the truth. Child rape murder was common. Young children, both boys and girls, were continually disappearing, and the fact that many of them were American and European was kept quiet by the press.

The degree of acceptability of anal sex between males (provided of course that one took the masculine role) seemed to vary according to social class and religious conviction. A great many Iranians, particularly among the lower classes, apparently regarded it as normal, especially before marriage. Many guys came the second time with one or more friends and enjoyed the sharing experience; it was obvious to me that, like so many 'straight' friends they often had the hots for each other and could express it only through a third person.

The more educated and wealthy classes did it too but tended to be more hypocritical about it. Society people pretended that sodomy did not exist in Iran and invariably said it was very bad. E.M. Forster notes in *A Passage to India* that behavior in the East is determined not by an internalized moral code but by social demands, in other words what one can get away with. As much emphasis as our society places on appearances, in comparison with Iranians we are open and honest.

In Iran you could bring home as many boys as you wanted, but when you started bringing home girls there was trouble—with the neighbors, the landlord, the girl's family, the police, everybody. Denial of access to girls is usually given as the main reason for the prevalence of homosexuality in countries like Iran. It was still very important for a girl to be a virgin on her wedding night, though it was only in the remote villages that an unmarried girl still risked death if she was discovered fornicating. Dating was on the rise while I was in Iran, but guys who were lucky enough to have sex with their girlfriends told me that it was usually the same kind of sex they had with me. I was also told that many married men continued to prefer anal sex.

Cocksucking was more frowned upon than fucking, though enjoyed almost as much. Many Iranians had no use for it, however, especially since sex with them was so often over before it really seemed to get started. They regarded oral sex as a perversion introduced by the West.

There was prostitution in Iran including a large enclosed red light district in Tehran, known as 'New City.' But whether for economic, hygienic, or other reasons, prostitutes certainly did not satisfy all the needs of all the males in a sprawling city of five million, where anonymous contact was quick and easy.

Religion enforced the emphasis on virginity and the disapproval of prostitution, but it could also act as a deterrent to homosexual acts. The force of religion in the lives of Iranians—a religion that was to ferment a revolution—impressed me greatly and often intruded on my life, including my sex life, in curious ways. I occasionally met a boy who would not do anything with anyone, male or female, because of religious scruples. Once I asked someone I had previously made it with to come home with me for a drink, but he said drinking and lovemaking that night were a sin for him because of a religious holiday. Another boy wondered what God would do to him after the first time he had sex, which was during the holiest part of the holy month of Ramadan. Another insisted on turning a tiny souvenir carpeting on my wall around so that the name of Allah, which was written on it, would not be facing us while we were naked in bed.

Frustration, of which there was plenty in Iran, had an economic as well as a sexual side. Stealing and hustling were all too often an integral part of a liaison, though your guests need not have been sex partners in order for them to take something when your back was turned. Stealing was so prevalent among all classes that a pathological disturbance, something far deeper than economic need, must have been behind it.

Add political frustration, and a composite picture begins to emerge. I like to single out the following of numerous similar experiences to illustrate that picture: Once I picked up a little soldier named Nasser and took him home, where we drank a lot of wine, did a lot of talking, and had a lot of sex. He told me that he was a poet and had been in jail for more than a year for writing a poem that he regarded as personal but that the government regarded as political. He told of the time he went to a professor and asked for his help in educating him, but since he was poor the prof told him to go away. Like so many young Iranians, he wanted to leave Iran and go to America if possible. I told him about the poet Reza Baraheni, whom I had read about in *Time*. After being imprisoned and tortured as a suspected subversive, Baraheni went to the States, where his book, *God's Shadow Prison Poems*, was translated and published. Nasser also spoke of an American friend he had had an affair with who wanted to take him to America but was killed in an accident. All he had left of him was a picture. He went on and on about being poor and living in a land in which there was no opportunity or hope for the poor. When I first came to Iran I could not see how Sadegh Hedayat's classic novel *The Blind Owl*, with its surrealistic outpouring of frustration, world-hatred and schizophrenic escapism, was characteristic of the Iranian mentality, but after four years I finally began to realize that it was.

While I was in Iran the country was rapidly losing its traditional values. In their stead came an enterprising and greedy middle class, university-educated women, blue jeans, the Rolling Stones, reckless drivers, monstrous traffic jams, air pollution, and bad manners. Western technology was moving in with its inevitable cultural baggage.

Western gay men, like Western technology, filled a need in rapidly developing Iran. The large American and European presence there, as well as the exposure of thousands of Iranian college and university students to the West, reminded Iranians of everything they wanted and, except for a fortunate few, did not have—economic well-being, educational opportunity, political rights, and sexual freedom. They had lived deprived lives for centuries, but now they were suddenly made aware of their frustrations. Westerners had a combined sexual, economic, and political appeal for Iranians. Because Western gay men provided the often needed secrecy (being an outsider who did not know the language and could not blab to friends and family) and availability (after all, someone had to take the scorned feminine role), they fitted in very nicely. If they had light hair and skin, all the better, for these features were in high demand.

Iran likewise had considerable appeal for us. Whatever our fantasies—cops, truck drivers, students, athletes, sailors, businessmen, gang bangs with masculine types—Iran was the place where we were likely to act them out, and with some of the most extraordinarily good-looking men and boys anywhere in the world.

I do not mean to imply that all my relations with Iranian males were merely sexual, though many of them were. I also developed friendships and emotional attachments with some pretty wonderful individuals. I think it was especially the loners and misfits who sought us foreigners out for more than just sex. A woman would not do, for Iranian men cannot look at women in terms of friendship. Unfortunately, a long tradition of separation of the sexes insured a considerable amount of mutual distrust and hostility between men and women.

Much of the physical satisfaction, too, was non-sexual, since in Iran kissing and holding hands are considered part of normal behavior between friends. Friendship is much more highly valued than it is here, and much more intimate.

Clearly the Iranian attitude towards the gay foreigner, as to foreigners in general and Americans in particular, was ambivalent. Envy, nationalism, and moralistic disapproval created a counterpoint to the obvious fascination Iran had with the U.S. The world has seen the vehemence with which Iran terminated its love affair with America and Americans, a vehemence not really surprising in any love-hate relationship.

Now I wonder: How are all those beautiful black-haired boys getting along without us?

The Persian Boy Today

David Reed

For those who picture Tehran as another Middle Eastern mud-house metropolis, let me repaint the picture. Thick-walled mud houses exist; they used to be the coolest thing going before air conditioning. But steel-and-glass office and apartment towers now dominate the city. Snowcapped mountains belie the image of barren desert. Trees and gardens are as plentiful in the city as in its carpet designs. Cars clog Tehran's broad modern avenues just as donkey carts used to clog its dirt roads. Tehranis even joke that the villagers new to the city life drive cars as they did their donkeys, only now they spew smog and they crash. A car is an Iranian man's phallic totem, a symbol of his macho ego. Every red light gives a chance for a Le Mans lunge and ego race. Traffic accidents probably exceed heart disease in Tehran's death statistics.

But the pent-up aggression released in traffic also finds release in sex. Government efforts to the contrary, Iran remains a Muslim, manly world. Women, native or foreign, rank a low second on the social totem pole. Women embody the forbidden fruit of sex whether they wear Paris fashion or Persian 'Čador' shrouds. Holy law forbids premarital intercourse, so both sexes are hung up on frustration of desire versus risk of punishment. Insatiable cravings explode in aggression. Movies of Italian bikini beauties excite young men to jeer women on the streets and to openly molest the unescorted.

Western women make especially vulnerable targets. Magazines and movies have labeled them as able and illegal.

"A man can't be blamed for his lust," they figure. In more primitive times Persians had other outlets for sexual release. Men denied the pleasure of women could turn to sheep—or other men. The former is now considered unmodern, the latter, illegal. But today American men get the cruisy eye once reserved for the cutest sheep.

Ironically, Iranians joke about American men in the same way we joke about Greeks—or Iranians. They say American men like to take it in the ass. Note the semantic subtlety: Iranian men fuck, an act that preserves their macho self-image; they say American men like to *get* fucked, so they are unmanly, effeminate, queer. And certainly not worthy of respect.

Bisexuality may run rampant in every country between Greece and Afghanistān, but its purpose is historically non-gay. A man does not desire another man, Allah forbid. If anything he desires a boy—a slim, hairless, effeminate youth. And he calls it sex education and birth control. When the boy becomes a man, he will turn his sexual sights to women and possibly boys, but not men. The tradition survives. The taboos persist. Islam condemns sodomy between consenting adults. Iran punishes it with severe jail sentences. Foreign jokes aside, Moslem law does not prescribe cutting off the penises of perverts as it does the hands of robbers. Anyway, Iran has long since banned eye-for-eye punishments. But Iranian jails are no joke. Nor are the infamous SAVAK secret police or their informers. Big Brother is watching.

Paranoia pervades what little public gay life exists in Tehran. Even under night's protective darkness the city parks feel as panicky as New York subway tearooms. Muggers are no threat. Street crime seems limited to minor brawls and assaults on women. Tehran could be the safest city in the world—for men. But for gay men it is one of the most frustrating.

I first discovered the frustration when a 28-year-old wrestler named ʿAbbās invited me home for sex. His hospitality was extremely rare, since most young Iranians cannot afford their own apartment; they stay with family until marriage. ʿAbbās led me to the corner of his street. He told me to wait there until he got inside the house; a neighbor could make hot gossip of a foreign man coming home with him. When I entered he locked the doors, drew the drapes, and turned on the television—loud. He would not strip completely for fear his family might drop in. Sure enough, they did. I was out the back door as they unlocked the front.

Iranians surround themselves with the social security of family and friends. Sex follows the same pattern. When one Iranian meets a receptive foreign gay, he will bring his friends the next time. ʿAbbās was a unique exception. Knowing him proved the difficulty of any gay relationship in Iran. Many a foreigner has known the ecstasy of an orgy followed by the agony of a robbery. One Iranian brings his sex-starved friends to visit. While a couple of them get their rocks off anally and orally with their host, another rummages through the apartment for cameras, loose money, or even Levi's (they sell for $50 a pair). One Texan I knew would lock everything in his closets and welcome legions. Others were less lucky.

A San Franciscan wearing a flashy mylar jumpsuit picked up a young Iranian in Tehran's only gay bar. When he went to work the next day, so did the Iranian. After picking the apartment's lock, he picked the best of its contents, including the silver jumpsuit. Another American caught his Iranian lover pocketing trinkets and, later, treasures from his well-appointed apartment. It says something about love and money in Iran. Love fits better in Persian poetry than in Iranian living. Homosexual love hardly exists there, at least with foreigners, without some price tag on it: free meals, free jeans, or possibly help in getting a U.S. visa. The foreigner always pays. And why should he not, thinks the Iranian, he is earning $30,000 a year.

One-night stands have their costs, too. In terms of pride, an Iranian will usually insist on playing the dominant 'masculine' role so as not to degrade himself by being passively 'feminine.' He will frequently also ask for money in order to claim that the sex was less for lust than for business. He can usually be talked out of demanding the money. Somehow just the asking for it seems enough for him to deny that there was any sin or sexual intimacy. Travelers to Iran must remember to bargain in the bedroom as well as in the bazaar. Otherwise they will not only be fucked like sheep but fleeced like them, too. But that can happen anywhere to any tourist. The place I did not expect it to happen was at the Chelsea Pub, the one only truly gay bar in Tehran.

The Chelsea Pub atop the Bel Air Hotel is the bar Tehran's foreign gays hate to love: expensive drinks with cheap liquor, ugly English chessboard decor, and a closed-circuit, none-too-candid camera scanning the room. But except for private parties, it is the only gay oasis in town. I decided I could live without the Bel Air the night a bartender pulled the old "but you only gave me a five" line and then pushed my change from a twenty into his pockets. Caveat emptor.

Fortunately, there are more honest and direct ways to meet and mate in Tehran. The streets are *the* place. A simple smile will lead to quick success on the sidewalks of Shah Reza or Pahlavi Avenues and, at sundown, in the city park where they intersect. It also works along the woody walks in Park Farah below the Intercontinental Hotel. Soldiers are infamous for out-of-uniform action. Most interesting and instant is the Wienerwald, a beer and snack bar near Tehran University. Hot and horny students pack the place. Beer lowers their inhibitions.

It was a hot summer night when two Wienerwald drinkers began a verbal tug-of-war for my affections. Soon their friends joined the argument, in which my preference was never consulted. Within minutes a *Gunsmoke* saloon slugout was in progress. I ducked under the bar just in time to dodge the first flying beer bottle. While bottles shattered against walls and patrons' heads, the bartender told me with a laugh that it happens all the time. Then the hunkier of the two original fighters bustled me out to a waiting motorcycle, and we left the glass-throwing menagerie behind.

A far more tranquil and traditional Persian social scene is found in Tehran's public baths. They are not gay; some even turn away foreigners on that suspicion. But they can be the friendliest pastime in town. Backgammon is popular in the sauna, sex games in the massage rooms or private bath closets. Someone, though, should rewrite the *Spartacus* international guidebook. The Villa Bath that it recommends has let suck-sex go to its head. I knew it the day my bath attendant dropped his waistcloth to reveal his penis still dirty from a previous customer; he said that for seven dollars he would fuck me. I decided bathing alone would be more fun. Far better and brighter is the Versailles Hotel Bath on Pahlevi Avenue: clean and congenial, with two handsome masseurs who give home service after hours in Mark Spitz bathing suits (removable) for $15. That is a good price in a city where lunch costs $10. But even the Versailles is in no way gay. Lots of looking, little touching, lots of sexual steam in the air going nowhere. And such is the myth of gay Iran. Hot air.

But do not give up. There is still that $ 30,000 a year job and there is still a chance for a semi-sexual life. Men with beards will improve their gay sex life by shaving. Remember that Iranians, many of whom sport beards, want female surrogates for sex. I did not shave, but I learned almost fatally to modify my sexual style. It happened with a friendly parking-lot attendant whom I had met on several nights in his little parking-lot shack. What began as a friendly tussle for position ended with a knife against my neck. His smile had vanished. He ordered me to let him up and then to lie down. He did what he wanted to do and curtly told me to leave. I had insulted his manhood by trying to usurp it.

Part of the problem is the Moslem code of cleanliness. More than once a sex partner asked me how I could do such a dirty, demeaning thing. When I would ask, "Well what were *you* doing?" he would respond, "But I was the man." Iranian Moslems will share a common cup at modern water fountains with no thought of germs. But they wash themselves and their clothes religiously. After sex men often wrap their penis in toilet tissue. The only explanation I ever got was the *Qur'ān* admonishes a man to wash his pants after sex if his 'dirty' penis touches them. Since jeans are always dry-cleaned and pressed with a crease in Iran, that ounce of toilet-tissue caution saves a pound of laundry care.

Such are the contrasts of modern Iran. Traditional morals in transitional upheaval. Desire fighting guilt. And money the lubricant that makes it excusable. Most frustrating for foreign gays is the contrast between the Persian male's display of open-chested shirts and tight-assed pants with his deeply ingrained repression and paranoia. In a sexual encounter Iranians rarely kiss, and even more rarely on the lips, never with the tongue unless they went to UCLA for a while. When it comes to oral sex, they find it better to receive than to give. And when they *do* get involved, they often literally "come and go", zip sip. As one American commented to me, "They used to fuck *with* sheep now they fuck *like* sheep." In all fairness I cannot generalize beyond my own experience. My experience, however, was as broad as that of any foreigner I met in Tehran, so I will stand by it.

Upper-class and diplomatic circles in Tehran are a world the typical American working there will never penetrate. Iranian students home from American universities will hold out for a Californian girl; those I met considered homosexuality as backward as camels. That leaves working-class young men, soldiers, and some Iranian students. It helps to learn Persian. It helps more to learn abstinence. While gay sex becomes an accepted modern lifestyle in the States, it smacks of primitive regression in Iran; a bad, lower-class habit. And a punishable offense.

A friend of mine in the American Embassy there takes every vacation he can to fly to Mykonos or Munich. He thought Tehran would be hell for straights but heaven for gays. The reason for his disappointment becomes clear in the way an Iranian trick approaches a pile of sex magazines on a coffee table. He will pick up *Playboy*, never *Playgirl*. He will turn to photos of women's rear ends, a favorite Persian turn-on and good birth control, too. He will point to the woman, and he will point to you. He does not ask if you *like* her; he asks if you will *be* her. It is either that or Mykonos or, better yet, good old New York. I hope my friend believes me.

Tehran: Dangerous Love

Hélène Kafi
Arno Schmitt (translator)

Tehran. The last days of August. It is terribly hot. Akbar cannot bear the heat any more. For hours he errs through the sinuous lanes of the Amīr ʿAbad quarter; there are only a few dry trees, gray concrete houses—many destroyed in the last Irāqī air raids. All this under the watchful eyes of a huge H̲umainī portrait on the wall of an unused factory building faded in the sun, covered by the dust of war.

Akbar makes the rounds. He would give a lot to get rid of this label "first mignon of Reza *bače bāz*" (Reza, the boy buggerer). Yes, to finish with this! He waits for Alī, his only friend from high school.

Akbar left school in order to evade military service. Chased by the Revolutionary Guard he had to allow Reza to take care of him. Reza is in his fifties, a clever bazaar and black market merchant with connections in the Revolutionary Guards—thanks to the gifts his wealth allows him to make.

Akbar, without a living soul to help him, could not refuse such a friend. Reza used to pick his boys in front of boys' schools; the imperial police knew and once, in 1967, he went to prison for corruption of minors. Since then he is generally called *baše bāz*. Right after the revolution, during the crazy campaigns against enemies of God, he repented publicly. Thanks to his penitence, his atonement, his gifts, he escaped the hands of H̲alh̲alī, then Public Prosecutor of revolutionary justice, now a member of parliament, who is said to have had 100 to 200 homosexuals executed in 1981/1982.

There was a drug dealer, 45, who had raped a boy of 17, whose incisors he had pulled out to heighten the pleasure; he was executed by firing squad—and the boy with him.

Reza was not as bad as that and he had to be discreet. He could not wait any more in front of the schools; he could not cruise any more. Now he had to send out others to recruit for him. They spotted Akbar: a pretty boy of 15, milk white skin, from northern Irān. And he was in trouble, and needed a protector.

Once his papers were in order, Reza took him in as an apprentice in his black market food wholesale business. Of course Akbar ended up in his bed. Akbar had left his family and he lived in a studio his "friend" had arranged. But the honeymoon came to an end. As Reza became brutal, Akbar really had enough of it. But how was he to fend for himself in a country where sodomy and prostitution are forbidden and punished with stoning?

Akbar: "I will volunteer for the front."

Ali looked disconcerted, pale faced, hollow-cheeked.

"No need to go to the front in order to commit suicide," he replied. "And even if you don't die, you know what you'll get out of it. You will be fucked by dozens of Rezas, sex hungry, violent, ferocious."

Everybody in Tehran heard the stories about rape in prisons and at the front, sordid stories about "special torturers" the authorities place in the cells of political prisoners. About forty strong rough criminals known to be rapists have been recruited by the mullahs to rape the enemies of the revolution. The best known is 'Crazy Husain'; he 'works' in Raš, in northern Irān.

And there is Arnuš, a young Armenian soldier with green eyes, buggered by an army of Revolutionary Guards in deepest Ḥuzistān; he had to be transferred several times to military hospital, then back to the local headquarters, and back to hospital. A physician of the regular army recently in Paris confirms the existence of the problem: "By the way soldiers are starting to worry about AIDS. Some colleagues have detected the disease among marines in Bandar Abbas (officially Bandar Humainī) on the Gulf."

Homosexuality, an ancient practice in Irān, has taken the most horrid forms under the mullahs. Those openly gay are executed, but a blind eye is turned on the religious colleges, traditional centers of male-male love. Alas the times of Hafiz are gone. No great poet around to sing the praise of boys.

During the last years under the Šah, fucking of young boys (who were not asked whether they liked it) slowly gave way to western style homosexuality. In 1977 all Tehran twaddled about the marriage of a painter and a musician. Today it is out of the question to advertise one's 'abnormal and anti-Islāmic' likings. But even the blindest and most savage repression cannot change human nature . . . and the lack of freedom, the renewed seclusion of women, the poor economy push hundreds of Akbars to illegal prostitution, turn soldiers into rapists, and force homosexual artists into exile—physically or spiritually.

In the Irān of the holy men nothing is holy, certainly not sexuality—neither homo nor hetero.

Turkey on the Brink of Modernity: A Guide for Scandinavian Gays

Mehmet Ümit Necef

You are into gay tourism. After the big hits like San Francisco, Amsterdam, Paris, and the usual Mediterranean countries, you want to try something new, an exotic place. You have met many men from that country in European streets and perhaps even at work, but rarely in gay bars—once in a while in parks and toilets, if you are into that.

You had an ambivalent attitude towards the ones you had sex with (if you ever had). On the one hand, you felt the attraction of the exotic, of the strange. And most of them underline their masculinity—they match well with your E. M. Forster- or O. Wilde-like preference for primitive and rough virility. On the other hand, you hesitated because you did not understand what exactly these guys were up to.

Although you may feel that "we gays especially have to be understanding and accepting," you have the typical Scandinavian reservation about anybody from "south of the Alps." And you heard many things from friends who had been there: "They are all bisexual. You can go to bed with any one of them, if you just know how"; "They must be paid for it, otherwise they get a bad conscience," etc.

If you have ever had a conversation with one of these dark guys, you might have noticed some general characteristics: irritation about personal questions; unease being in a gay bar or an obvious cruising area; the man you converse with declares himself to be heterosexual and stresses that he is married. If you ended up in bed with him, you probably also noticed that he had difficulty in playing both the 'active' and the 'passive' roles.

Anyhow, you take the plane to İstanbul. With the help of your gay guide, you meet a sweet local guy on the beach.

You are struck by the traffic chaos, the poverty of some parts of town, and the abundance of armed soldiers in the street; but you are here "only for gay tourism." Wandering in the streets or drinking the famous coffee or strong tea in one of the countless coffeeshops, you notice that most of the people around are men.

Only men were at the football stadium where you once went with your new Turkish friend. Most action on the field was accompanied by violent shouting and 'war dances.' After a while you notice a certain slogan which nearly half the crowd shouts each time one of the referees makes a decision against one of the teams: "*Ibne hakem.*" You ask your friend what it means. He answers, a bit embarrassed; "It means queer or fag referee." You get confused; the referee looks 'perfectly normal.' "Is he really homosexual?" you inquire. Your friend calmly explains: "I don't know, but that's not the point. Because if somebody gets angry at someone and wants to curse him, he calls him *ibne*. He can even call a woman *ibne kari*, meaning 'queer bitch.'"

In descriptions of how the homosexual role and identity developed in Western Europe and the USA in the last hundred years, a question always hangs in the air: How did people who loved and made sex to people of their own sex conceptualize themselves and how did society define them before the middle of the nineteenth century? We have documents about ancient Greeks and Romans and we know a lot about the last hundred years, but the vast period in between is largely unexplored.

I think that investigating homoeroticism of countries like Turkey can contribute to understanding the situation in pre-industrial Western Europe. This is not to say that Turkey is not already partially industrialised or that Turks are not influenced by Western culture. Out of a people of 50 million, 3 million work in industry; half the population lives in towns, a third live in cities of over a million. But in many of its social, economic, and cultural traits Turkey still resembles early nineteenth century Europe. A weak women's movement and the lack of a gay movement are only two of these similarities.

THE ROLES OF IBNE *AND* KULAMPARA

The word "homosexual" entered Turkish by translations from European languages: first as *homoseksüel*. During the turkification of the language after the foundation of the republic in 1923 the work *eşcinsel* (equal-sex-ual) was coined, but this did not fit the roles and identities in Turkey and confusion arose.

The existing roles for sexual relations between men were *ibne* and *kulampara*. An *ibne* is an effeminate man who exclusively plays the 'passive' role in the sexual act. He does not marry, because he is (thought to be) impotent. An *ibne* can be a transvestite—earning his living by dancing, singing, or prostituting himself.

To be an *ibne* is the worst thing a man can be. Simply because he accepts being fucked 'like a woman' and moves and speaks in an unmanly manner.

So it may come as a surprise that the most popular (male) singers are transvestite *ibneler*. One of them, Bülent Ersoy, underwent an operation and is now a woman. Turks explain their admiration for these artists by pointing to their artistic talent and to the fact that nearly all artists are crazy and strange. All these singers interpret heterosexual love songs (though in some cases the sex of the loved one is unclear) and even act in films as straight lovers. The word *ibne* is derived from the arabic *ubna* meaning 'the sickness of liking to get fucked.'

The other role is played by the *kulampara* (from the Persian *ġulām-pāre*, 'fucker of boys') or *oğlanci*, 'having to do with boys.' A *kulampara* is over 16 and nearly always married, like all men—you are expected to marry after military service at the latest. But because of the 'bride price' still due in rural Turkey some poor peasants marry later.

In contrast to *ibne, kulampara* does not constitute a special type of man. Any married man 'too full of lust' or separated too long from his wife looks for prostitutes, mistresses, animals (dogs and donkeys) or *ibneler*. Nobody would consider himself as 'abnormal,' 'perverse,' 'sinful,' let alone 'homosexual' for fucking an *ibne*. He would not identify himself with a (minority) group of 'men-fuckers' or 'animal-fuckers.' To bugger an *ibne* is an enjoyment open to all; any man could be seduced by one of those.

BEFORE MARRIAGE

In Turkey it is important that the first wife is a virgin. If she dies or gets divorced, the man may marry a widow or a divorcée. Polygamy is officially forbidden and rare. That means that an unmarried man cannot go to bed with an unmarried woman. If he does, they must marry afterwards.

Conversations with Turkish men show that sexual play with other men plays a rather important role in young men's sex life, especially in rural areas. While still young, playing the 'passive' role apparently does not disturb them unduly. After marriage most men are exclusively heterosexual.

THE HOMOSEXUAL ROLE AND IDENTITY

In spite of all this the role and identity of 'homosexual' exists—in the big cities at least. For individuals to develop the role and identity of 'a homosexual' and for society to recognize it, to accept it in whatever manner, a certain social climate is required. The big cities with less rigid control by family and neighbors (a certain anonymity), less personal dependence, more reliance on impersonal society (social security instead of family or patron), and more privacy offer this climate.

Life in rural areas does not leave room for the development of individuality; almost everything is predetermined. A Turk thinks and is thought of in relation to other people and groups. He is the son of a father and a mother, whom he addresses as *baba* and *anne* (or *ana*) all his life. It would be inconceivable for Turks to call their parents by name. They are also expected to add the words "abi" or "abla" to the names of their elder brothers and sisters to show respect. Parents seldom leave room for initiative. A parent asking a child which ice cream it wants is very exceptional.

To put it bluntly: a Turkish boy grows up under the wings of his elder family members, marries the woman recommended by them, works industriously for his family, fights fanatically for his cause, and dies bravely for his country and flag.

But 'City Turks' are developing a concept of "Self/Ego" similar to that found in Northern Europe. Some cities have a homosexual subculture with discotheques, bars, beaches, etc.—but even compared with Greece it is underdeveloped.

One typical aspect of the Turkish scene is the importance of role playing: some men acting or dressing up like women and others underlining their masculinity. It is still *ibne* and *kulampara* rather than of 'gays.' Transvestism plays a much bigger role in Turkey (and Southern Europe) than in the North or the USA. This seems to be the result of relations between the sexes. Turkish men and women almost live in two different worlds. The homosexuals are just aping the 'normal' world.

The Dawn of a Gay Movement in Turkey

Jehoeda Sofer

Turkey is the most Westernized country in the Muslim world; it is the most industrialized; it has a strong middle class; and it has an urban gay subculture. In the late 1970s the gutter press announced every now and then the foundation of a gay organisation.[1] Bülent Ersoy, one of Turkey's most popular singers, if not the most popular, was often named as a possible leader of such an organisation.

The September 12, 1980 military coup d'état brought all attempts to found a gay organisation to a halt. The generals suppressed every progressive movement and campaigned for conservative morals. Transvestites, transsexuals, and homosexuals were among the victims of this campaign. But as soon as the generals loosened their control, some gay men took the initiative. The oppression may even have stimulated gay politics.

In July 1986 Dr. Arslan Yüzgün published *Türkiye'de Eşcinselik, dün bugün* (i.e., Homosexuality in Turkey, Yesterday and Today), and in 1987 an organized group of homosexuals was set up within the Democratic Radical Union Party.

POLICE HARASSMENT

"A scene at the toilet in İstanbul's Taksim Park. In the dark, a police car stops, five or six policemen get out of the car and enter the toilet, collect everybody who is there, kick, hit, insult, push them into the cars, and drive to the police station. Two, three days detention. . . . The position of the homosexuals in Ankara and Izmir is even worse. . . . There the police even control the homes.

They arrest you at your own home. On the slightest suspicion they inform your parents, and laughing in their faces, tell them that their son is a homosexual."[2]

Police harassment is mainly directed against effeminate men, transvestites, and transsexuals. They are taken to police stations, photographed, their heads are shaven, fingerprints and blood are taken. Some are exiled to a provincial town—especially male prostitutes. Masculine looking men are left alone.[3]

After the military takeover this police practice became more systematic. Since sexual activities between males are not prohibited in the Turkish Penal Code (*Türk Ceza Kanunu* of 1926), the harassment was justified by the Law on Police Duties and Powers (*Polis Vazife ve Salahiyet Kanunu*) of 1934, and by articles of the Penal Code prohibiting transvestism, prostitution, or activities considered to be against public morality.

In June 1981 the military regime, popular as a result of effective combating of terrorism, prohibited performances by transsexuals (like Bülent Ersoy), by transvestites, and by effeminate men (like Zeki Müren).[4] The ban was lifted in January 1988.

In June 1985, a new Clause (5f) added to the Law on Police Duties and Powers gave the police greater powers against "persons whose behavior is against morality and public customs." Although homosexuality was not mentioned in the law, the Home Minister Yildirim Akbulut said during the parliamentary debate: "The new law . . . empowers us to arrest people suspected of homosexuality for a term of 24 hours . . . We don't believe that homosexuality is not one of the anti-social tendencies. We have to be tough against persons who have such perverted thoughts and tendencies. The number of such persons increases daily. They became the cancer of society. No segment of our society approves people who hold such thoughts and tendencies . . . We therefore shall introduce measures against these people everywhere, but especially in the big cities."[5]

ARSLAN YÜZGÜN

Sexuality was until recently not a subject of discussion. The gutter press started writing about sex, with sensational stories, insinuating headlines, and nude photographs. The more sophisticated press 'discovered' sexuality only later, and not before the publication of books on sexuality written by religious fundamentalists (for example: Ali Riza Demircan, *Islama Göre Cinsel Hayat* [i.e., Sexual Life according to Islam], İstanbul 1985). Rock Hudson's death from AIDS in 1985 drew attention to sexuality in general and homosexuality in particular.

In July 1986 Dr. Arslan Yüzgün, an economist, published his *Homosexuality in Turkey*. The book was classified as detrimental to youth and thus could only be sold in a sealed plastic bag. Yüzgün later published another two books: *Uçurum* (i.e., The Abyss), a film script on a man who was fired because of his homosexuality,[6] and *Mavi Hüviyetli Kandilar* (i.e., Pink Identity Card), short stories on transvestites.[7] The importance of *Homosexuality in Turkey* lies in the fact that this is the first serious publication on (male) homosexuality. Yüzgün's aim was mainly political: putting the issue of gay rights on the agenda. The popular papers were scandalized by Yüzgün's suggestion that in Istanbul alone there are more than half a million homosexuals and in Turkey more than two million (Turkey's population is about 55 million). Much attention was paid to homosexuality and to Yüzgün himself, a not unwelcome side effect. The book proved to be a best seller.

Although Yüzgün defines a homosexual as a person who is attracted to members of the same sex, he sometimes slips into the traditional equation of homosexual equals fuckee; e.g., he says: "In Turkey there are hundreds of thousands, even millions, of men who boast they are *kulampara*." But these are not included in his research which is based on a questionnaire conducted among 223 male homosexuals. On the selection of the participants in the research Yüzgün says: "I knew they were homosexuals."[8] He found them all in İstanbul, more precisely in Beyoğlu, İstanbul's red light district, one of the few areas in the Middle East where a visible gay subculture exists complete with bars, discos, and prostitution.

Although only representative for a limited area, I would like to give some figures published. Thirteen and nine-tenths percent said they had sex with males before they were ten, and 37.7% said they had sex between 11 and 15. A remarkably high percentage of 82.1

said they do not regard their homosexuality as a problem. Although 56.5% have a problem telling friends or family, 39.9% said their parents knew about their homosexuality; of these 80.4% (32.1% of all parents) accepted the homosexuality of their sons as an unchangeable fact. And 55.2% still live with their parents.[9]

GAY ORGANISATION

No doubt, Yüzgün's activities mobilized homosexuals and opened the way for the foundation of a gay organisation. In spring 1987, the Turkish Green Radical Union Party was founded as a federation of atheists, anti-militarists, environmentalists, and feminists. Homosexuals played an important role; e.g., Ibrahim Eren, Ali Poyrazoğlu, and Melih Ergen, who in May 1987 organised a hunger strike by thirty-five homosexuals in Istanbul and Ankara against police behavior.[10] This all led to an unprecedented action by the state television when on June 16, 1987, a program on homosexuality was broadcast under the title *Kronik Bunalim* (Chronically Disturbed). The hunger strike remained marginal, receiving little support from homosexuals, and thus ended without concrete achievements.

The Party newspaper *Yeşil Baris* (i.e., Green Peace) has a gay page. In December 1988, party leader Eren and the paper's editor Abdul Kadir Demir Özu were charged with spreading obscene material by publishing a translation of a poem by Meliagos (seventh century B.C.), a photo of two nude youths, and an article about the homosexuality of famous personalities, including the founder of the Turkish Republic, Kemal Atatürk.[11]

NOTES

1. Fred de Ceunnick van Chapelle, Een Turks fenomeen in Amsterdam, in *sek* 7/83. p. 27.

2. Arslan Yüzgün, *Turkiyede eşcinselik, dün bügün*, İstanbul: Hüryüz, 1986; I want to thank Kemal Ali for translating.

3. *Waar Turkije ophoudt man te zijn* in *Turkÿe Krant*, April 1983, Nijmegen. pp. 24-30; cf. *Turkey Begins Campaign against Homosexuality* in *The New York Times*, May 7, 1981.

4. Frans G. van Hasselt, *Turks verbood op travestie treft de populairste artiesten* in *NRC-Handelsblad*, July 25, 1981.

5. Frans G. van Hasselt, *Politiwet stelt Turkije in staat . . .* in *NRC-Handelsblad*, August 28, 1985.

6. Arslan Yüzgün, *Uçurumlik*, İstanbul: Hüryüz, 1987.

7. Arslan Yüzgün, *Mavi Hüvigetli Kandilar*, İstanbul: Hüryüz, 1987.

8. Yüzgün said this during a workshop of the "Homosexuality, Which Homosexuality" conference in the Vrije Universiteit, Amsterdam, December 1987.

9. Jale Şimşek, *Turkey, a Country with a long homosexual history*, in *Second ILGA Pink Book*, Utrecht, 1988. pp. 153-161.

10. Jehoeda Sofer, *Homobeweging naar Westers model omdat Turkije een Westers-land* is in *De Gay Krant* 101, February 27, 1988. p. 17.

11. Can Istanbullo, *Turkish gays to face trial*, in *ILGA-Bulletin*, 5-6. 1988. p. 2.

Transvestites and Transsexuals in Turkey

Thijs Janssen
Peter op't Veldt (translator)

This paper is mainly based on conversations with four transvestites, twelve women who had been men, and five men accompanying them. First I give a definition of some terms, then I will treat the history of transvestites, their self-image, the views of 'ordinary' Turkish men on them, their occupations, and their way of life.

TERMINOLOGY

'Transvestism' and 'transsexualism' were coined by Western medicine; 'transvestite' denoting a person feeling a strong urge to wear clothes of the other sex, 'transsexual' denoting someone with a continuous 'unsuppressible' feeling of belonging to the sex of which he/she does not possess the primary sexual organs.

In the dictionaries[1] 'transvestism' is translated as *alay, hiciv, karikatür*, and *taklit*, words meaning 'mockery,' 'caricature,' or 'imitation.' The (foreign) word *transseksüel* is heard much less than *köçek*, which used to denote 'a young dancer dressed like a woman,' but now covers both transvestites and transsexuals. In Turkey it is difficult to base a division on the desire for a sex-change operation, since all my transvestite informants confided to me that they would like to undergo sex change if it were not for the expense. They claimed that everybody in their circles shared this wish.

The *köçek* is regarded as very feminine, as a woman—albeit imperfect, because she cannot become a mother. And she has man's freedom of movement: almost a 'third gender.'

HISTORY

In what is now the Turkish Republic transvestism has a long history. The Ottoman sultans kept young dancers to perform in woman's clothes and sometimes were part of the sulṭān's or some rich paša's harem.

But the common people were not excluded: İstanbul is said to have harbored at least 600 *köçekler* in 1905[2]—earning their living in the taverns of the Galata district or as dancers at wedding parties and circumcisions. Performances in which the *köçek* assisted by musicians, acrobats, clowns, and jugglers were very spectacular. These showmen were organized into *kol*s; in the middle of the seventeenth century twelve *kol*s existed comprising some 3,000 dancers alone.[3]

The most popular dances satirized the manners and schemings of upper-class ladies. The clown played the role of the underhand lover, who—if accepted—took the woman out onto the floor making obscene gestures to the dancers and the audience. The *köçek* wore women's dress, i.e., veils, long vividly colored skirts, and metal adornments.[4]

Professional Dancing Dishonored and Made Popular

The popularity of the dancing boys led to so much trouble and quarreling among the Janissaries that finally, to preserve order in his army, Sultan Mahmud forbade their appearances. Many of them fled to Egypt, where they were employed by the Khedive Mehmet Ali Paşa. Finally, so as to put an end to the riots, there was a law passed in 1857 which outlawed *köçekler*, prohibiting their performances.[5]

The dancers' popularity found expression in a great number of poems singing their beauty and grace, especially by the seventeenth century author Enderunlu Fazil. Even taking the literary conventions of his time into account, Fazil's words betray an enormous admiration.

At the beginning of the nineteenth century Bartholdy[6] noticed that most *köçek* were Greek, Armenian, or Jewish and that a Turk would never want to have such an inferior profession. It was generally assumed that *köçek* could be buggered. This explains much of the excitement of the male spectators, many of whom courted the *köçek*. Most *köçek* were boys, some were castrated.

Although public performances of *köçek* were forbidden in 1857 they did not disappear. Male dancers still perform female dances during Anatolian village feasts.

The *transseksüel* can be seen as a modern *köçek*. Both wear the woman's clothes of their time; both work in showbusiness and prostitution; both are dishonored.

IMAGE

Hülya (boy's name: Murrat) Yilmaz, 24, told me:

> I am the youngest of five brothers. They live with my family in Çorum. When I was born my mother had hoped for a girl and consequently she treated me as one. She dressed me in girls' clothes, and I did not have to work in my father's company like my brothers. Instead I was allowed to stay home to read; I was to go to college. Everybody thought I was soft and girly, and from my twelfth year on I was fucked by elder nephews and boys from the neighborhood. This changed when I moved to Ankara to study medicine. Everyone knew I got fucked, but no one dared to talk about it. The only thing I noticed was that my father, brothers, and uncles often were very angry at me. I did not feel bad or anything. In Ankara I got to know two *köçekler* who became my dearest friends. At first I thought them strange but later on I realized I too was 'like that,' and I also wanted to be operated upon and to get beautiful breasts. They helped me with hormones, picked out some clothes for me, and brought me into contact with the surgeon. The only problem was the money. First I worked as a prostitute and later I asked my family for it, but I did not tell them what I needed it for. I wrote them later on, but they never answered my letters and I did not dare to go back. I had to quit my studies and it was very difficult to find a job. That is why I work as a prostitute, just like my friends. Sometimes we dance in a nightclub. I make a fair sum of money that way. I can dress reasonably, but often people abuse me.

Most of my *köçek*-informants come from upper-middle-class families and were raised in a protected environment. As children they used to wear girls' clothes which is common in Turkey as a protection against the 'evil eye.' (Girls' clothes—and their appreciation by the boys—should be seen as an explanation in retrospect rather than as the actual cause for their becoming *köçek*.) As children they kept away from their brothers' rough little games. Instead they stayed inside to help their mother. Often they were sexually abused[7] and often the boys were stigmatized as *ibne*, 'fucked one.' They took this with resignation. Between the ages of 16 and 18 they moved to a big city. Here they mixed with *köçek* who told them how easy it was to use hormones and to get operated. The decision to change their sex is seen by all of my informants as a logical consequence of earlier events. All asserted to have been born in the wrong body. The decision however was only taken when they had become friends of *köçekler*; this can be regarded as decisive, because other *köçekler* grant a certain legitimacy to their own behavior and help them to stand up in an ignorant, hostile environment.

One of the most important things for the *köçek* is her appearance and she will do everything in her power to look as feminine as possible. She has chosen to spend her life as a woman and this attitude can best be expressed by her appearance. Many *köçekler* are hardly distinguishable from biological women. But it is impossible for them to marry and they are unable to give birth.

WORK

Most companies and certainly most public institutions prefer women to *köçekler*; so most have to resort to entertainment and prostitution. (Anyhow, office work is not well paid.) The traditional job, dancing at parties, has lost much ground, whereas performing in clubs has assumed enormous proportions. Bülent Ersoy is the prime example of someone who has been very successful in showbusiness in spite of or maybe thanks to his change of sex. However, prostitution remains the most important source of income. Here appearance is important, because the lovelier a *köçek* looks, the more money she can make. They are not really happy with their lives and often jealous of women who have honorable jobs:

> I was educated well and last month I applied for a job as a cashier at the Osmanli Bakasi, but I was not hired because I am not a real woman. Ridiculous! At night I'm often preferred and I am not cheaper than other.

This was the grievance of a twenty year old *köçek* who boasted nobody could see that she used to be a man.

Since femininity is so important a lot of money and time is spent on it. The term 'transseksüel' is avoided carefully because it is associated with a former male identity and it puts the newly acquired femininity in an unfavorable light.

If they dressed in traditional Turkish clothes—i.e., long skirts or trousers, kerchief, no bare limbs—they had considerable trouble walking the streets and showing off their femininity. There are older unoperated *köçekler* who wear rather loose clothes to hide their male features; most of them no longer work as prostitutes. Many young *köçekler* try to conform to a western image of femininity, which is very popular in Turkey and which presents women as tempting and sexually accessible to every man. So they wear short skirts, tight jerseys, and high-heeled shoes; they dye their hair, use large quantities of make-up, and talk in a high pitched voice. Their posture and outfit is provocative. They distance themselves from generally accepted standards and turn to a different society, trying to show off their 'merchandise' as well as possible.

"GIRLFRIENDS"

In groups of four or five they go shopping, help each other to choose clothes, accessories, etc. Afterward they try everything on. These groups often share apartments and do a lot of things together. There is a great rivalry between the 'girls,' especially where appearances are involved. A vicious remark about hands or feet being too big or a beard too strong hurts a *köçek* and leaves her totally upset. Often the *köçekler* of one group work together as dancers or as prostitutes.

Most *köçek* cooperate with a man who protects them—normally a very masculine young man; he goes with them to town or on holiday, posing as the male relative guarding the respectable ladies of the family. According to Mürsel, 18, he normally does not get cash, the *köçek* pays his expenses, gives him small presents, and offers free sex.

Most *köçek* prostitutes work in the street. The customers sit waiting in their cars to pick one up. Most women prostitutes work in brothels. Their price is about 4,000 T£; the *köçekler'* price, about 6,000 T£. The *köçekler* explain the difference by saying that they are cleaner, because they do not menstruate. But I think that customers in cars can afford higher prices than those going to the more traditional brothel.

A lot of money is needed to keep their bodies in shape; many have to service the debt they incurred for the operation, which costs about 2,000,000 T£. The earlier they can manage to get the money, the more feminine they will look—and as women they do not have to do military service. Many borrow money with usurious interest. It takes them years to pay it all back. If they have wealthy families they will try to borrow the money from them under false pretenses. Compensation for military service (which is legally possible in Turkey) is a good reason and the amount required is similar to the costs of the operation.

The family is always an enormous problem. The *köçek*'s loss of status rubs off onto the family's honor. Renunciation is rather the rule than the exception.

> After I had my operation I tried to visit my family, but when my father and brother saw me they did not even want to talk with me and sent me away. They threatened to kill me if I would return, because I had disgraced the entire family. They did not answer my letters and refused to have anything to do with me.
>
> Yozgatt, 30

Not one of my informants maintained contact with her family and none thought the relationship could ever be restored to normal. *Köçek*s often feel humiliated, the object of mockery, rejected because of their nature, outsiders not being entitled to any status.[8] Some *köçek* regard this as a consequence of religion, as some *hadīṯ* forbid self-castration and transvestism.[9] But most of them do not attach much value to this view, it is said after all in the Qur'ān that not all people can be perfect, while others are quite indifferent to whatever Allāh and Muḥammed are supposed to have said.

As often with stigmatized groups most *köçekler* accept their inferiority—together with a certain pride, necessary to keep sane. They consider themselves as fit women, knowing that this is not the general opinion.

> I indeed look like a woman and I feel like one, but I am not a woman. I'm my own master and that is why I can do everything I like. Even if I sleep with a lot of men. I can lose my honor only once!
>
> Hülya Yilmaz, 24

TURKISH MEN'S IMAGE OF THE KÖÇEK

Most Turkish men do not understand why a man should give up his superior position to take up the role of woman. There is a great difference between men who know a *köçek* personally and those who do not, and attribute all kind of qualities to them.

> A *köçek* is funny. It has big hands and feet and sometimes even grows a beard. You always recognize it is a man really. It always has a lot of money. An ordinary man cannot afford an operation. It has its mind always on sex and tries to seduce normal men with money.

Seventeen year old Rüstem said he derived this wisdom from the newspapers. The press carries rather exceptional stories about *köçekler*, Bülent Ersoy and Zeki Müren in particular.

Twenty-six year old Atnan from Ankara who knows some *köçekler* has a completely different view:

> There are very beautiful transsexuals. Some are even better looking than real women, with real big breasts. Others are ugly of course. I picked up a prostitute once who turned out to be a *köçek*, but I sent her away. There are a lot of transsexuals who provide food, drinks, and even money to make love to men. I would never pay for it.

It is generally assumed that *köçekler* have a lot of money and that they spend it on men. While some *köçek* make good money in prostitution I did not meet even one man who admitted that he had ever paid a *köçek*, although almost all found it normal to pay a woman prostitute. The men who told me that they had sex with a *köçek* claimed to have been paid by her. Others said they would never have sex with a transsexual, because it was still a male, but without the honor of a man.

Many men think that *köçek* and *ibne* have so much in common that they belong to one category. Older men in particular believe that every *ibne* strives after a sex-change. This idea was not confirmed by the *ibneler* I met.

Many men welcome *köçek* working in nightclubs and in the street, because it diminishes the risk that their own daughters and sisters might dishonor them by working in this business. Police sometimes harass *köçek* on the ground that they endanger public morality.

SUMMARY

The terms 'transvestism' and 'transsexualism' are better not used. Although they are often mentioned in western literature, '*Köçek*' is a more adequate term and is the one used by the *köçekler* themselves.

In Turkey there is a long tradition of men not living as men, but as womanish dancers and singers. Throughout the ages there have been few changes in the *köçekler*' occupations. Whereas formerly, dancers could bring their public to ecstasy and some were the sultan's sweetheart, nowadays they are mostly mocked. In former days some boys—especially slaves—were forced to become *köçek*; now it is the decision of the *köçek* themselves.

The contemporary *köçek* regards herself as a woman and attaches a great value to a feminine appearance and her social acceptance as a woman. She takes liberties a respectable Turkish woman cannot take without being renounced or endangering her family's honor. The *köçek* cannot undermine anybody's honor (any more) since she has already been repudiated and has lost all honor as a result of her choice.

NOTES

1. The following were consulted: *Redhouse Elsözlügü*, İstanbul and *Oxford Türkçe-Ingilizce Sözlük*, Oxford English-Turkish Dictionary.

2. M. And, A *Pictoral History of Turkish Dancing*, Ankara: Dost Yayinlari Çankaya, 1976. pp. 139,140.

3. Ibid. pp. 141,142.

4. Ibid. pp. 139-141.

5. Ibid. p. 141—a.s.: Muḥammed ʿAlī was the 'autonomous' gouvenor of Egypt holding the title of *paša*, not of *hedive*.

6. Jakob L.Salomo Bartholdy (1779-1825), *Bruchstücke zur näheren kenntnis des heutigen Griechenlands*, Berlin: Realschul-Buchhandlung, 1805, pp. 292,3, 7,372-7; translation: A. du C. *Voyages en Grèce faits dans les annëes 1803 et 1804*, Paris: Dentu, 1807. II 80-80; cit. And p. 140.

7. All my informants have been raped, but this might happen to a lot of boys, who do not become *köçek*s.

8. Cf. N. Elias & J. Scotson, *The Established and the Outsider*, London: Frank Cass & Co., 1965. pp. 4-56. Their explanation fits the case of the *köçek* remarkably well, not the case of men having homosexual contacts.

9. James A. Bellamy, *Sex and Society in Popular Literature* in *Society and the Sexes in Medieval Islam* 1965. pp. 4-56. (ed. A.L. Sayyid-Marsot), Malibu, Calif.: Udena, 1979, pp. 30,31.

Not-So-Gay Life in Karachi: A View of a Pakistani Living in Toronto

Badruddin Khan

There is no "gay life" in Karachi in the Western sense of the word; there are no bars, no newspapers, and few instances of lovers living together. Just as predictably, sex between men occurs often and "friendships" develop that are just as committed and emotional as among gay lovers in New York. The deep differences, however, arise from tradition, history, the environment, and the culture and its expectations.

THE CITY OF KARACHI

Karachi is a large city of over eight million persons. As with the country as a whole, it is predominantly Muslim. Unlike other cities in Pakistan, however, it is extremely heterogeneous. At the airport, the immediately striking difference the visitor will observe in comparison to most other countries is the rich variety of dress. Ethnic groups include Sindhis, Punjabis, Pathans, and Baluchis, as well as the "Mohajir" group that collectively includes several additional ethnic groups. While it is nominally in the Sindh province, most of Karachi's residents are immigrants from other parts of the country and from India (at the time of the partition that created Pakistan in 1947), and speak regional languages in addition to Urdu, the national language.

Regional traditions extend beyond language; among Pathans, for example, sex between men and boys is common and accepted as a necessary release in the absence of women. Sir Richard Burton, famed researcher of things sexual, refers to an ancient Pathan proverb in his introduction to *Kama Sutra: The Hindu Art of Love-making*, a treatise that describes over 100 positions for lovemaking and includes a discussion of the role of masseurs: "Women for breeding, boys for pleasure, but melons for sheer delight." Since before the days of Alexander the Great, the peoples of this region have been recognized as pragmatists, who practiced war with ferocity and love with great dedication.

SOCIAL STRUCTURE

Pakistani society is based on fundamentalist communal precepts; its central institution is the biological family. The meaning and purpose of life has its root in loyalty to family, in protecting its honor and stature, in procreation, and in caring for children. While these values are common to most societies, in Pakistan they are the clear and unswerving raison d'être of life, and supersede individual desires and differences when there is conflict.

This results in life-styles and social values that are not conducive to a gay identity. Children live with their parents until they get married. It is virtually unheard of for an unmarried son to live in the same city as his biological family and yet live apart. Single men and women may live with their parents (even without economic need) through middle age and beyond. Even separate households function as social satellites, linked inexorably by biological bonds to the family center.

There is a very practical foundation to this focus on family. As with other traditional societies, it is "closed"; it is virtually impossible for a newcomer to enter economic or social life without an introduction. The family establishes one's station in life, which in turn sets boundaries for the aspirations of individuals. While these boundaries can be exceeded, "social status" is virtually impossible to change in just a generation or two, and does not naturally follow material success. This "tribal" model then requires that activities consonant with family-oriented goals be awarded the highest recognition.

The highest of these goals is clearly childbearing and childraising. Families devote themselves selflessly to caring for their young (and not so young) with a devotion that would be considered pathological in the West. Rather than temporary breeding grounds for children to grow up in before they move on to independence, families are like organisms that extend themselves by absorbing their young, and they grow stronger or weaker based on the contributions of the new entrants. This is not just one model of life in Pakistan; it is not a choice; it is the only way of life. Individual love is recognized only in the context of this environment, and it is supported only if it furthers its development. This applies to marriages, which are usually arranged. Whether husband and wife get along with each other is strictly secondary to whether they breed well. If a husband takes care of his family's security needs and bears many children, what he does for personal sexual satisfaction is uninteresting to everyone involved, so long as he is discreet. It is certainly not discussed. It simply does not matter. It is quite irrelevant and—so long as it is kept a private matter—tolerated. The "moral" issues of two men having sex, as in the West, do not arise in and of themselves.

The "acceptance" of extramarital homosexual liaisons should not be taken to imply that there is ready, good-humored indulgence in this regard. On the contrary, homosexual behavior is derided in public discourse. Pragmatic accommodations to individual tastes must of necessity be discreetly worked out. From the standpoint of "family," it is less risky for men to have affairs with other men than with women. In most social situations any direct discussion of homosexuality is strictly discouraged. Homosexual behavior is proscribed in the Quran; but infidelity with a woman may result in prescribed penalties that are far worse.

In this environment, homosexual sex is uninteresting, since it does not create children, nor does it add to the potential of children in the family's resource base (except to supplement the income of lower-class hustlers). In fact, sex in general is interesting primarily because of its impact on family, rather than its potential for individual pleasure or carnal fulfillment.

This interdependence between individuals and family is further exacerbated by the lack of widespread health insurance and social security benefits. The public health system is very poor and private hospitals are expensive. While companies often pay for employee health coverage, the individual without a steady job and without family ties finds himself precariously alone. In Pakistan, family support is literally a matter of life and death.[1]

THE GAY WAY

"Gay" implies a legitimation of a relationship that runs counter to family; therefore gay life does not exist in Pakistan in general, nor in Karachi in particular. From a practical standpoint, two lovers would find themselves without any social context. Unlike the fag-bashing response to same-sex relationships in the West, there is little such behavior here. There *is* no threat to family; there is, simply, irrelevance. At worst there is ridicule; at best, there is willful blindness to the situation.

Two lovers from different social classes would have to explain their togetherness at every juncture. If from the same social class, they would have to invent a family based "link" to justify their intimacy, such as: "I know him because he went to school with my brother, and he needed a place to stay, so we are living together." This might superficially appear to be the same as in the West; however, the closed and relatively immobile nature of society in Pakistan makes such simple solutions remarkably difficult to implement. Inevitably, the "cover" provided by the excuse would be blown; the resulting embarrassment would "shame the family" and destroy the relationship.

Further, the lack of privacy in most living situations makes a personal relationship that is outside the norm impossible to maintain. In poorer households, space is shared. In wealthier families, servants provide the ultimate monitoring system, and it is impossible to maintain secrecy. If secrecy is crafted nonetheless, it has the inevitable effect of isolating and destroying the very relationship it was intended to protect.

Preventing "shame" or otherwise embarrassing the family is the most basic requirement for respectability; respectability is the basic requirement for social acceptance; and social acceptance is the oxygen without which life ceases to exist in any meaningful way. Therefore, the most enlightened Western-educated, liberal-radical, gay liberationist finds himself immobilized on return to the Motherland. To agitate would be to bite the hand (family) that feeds. To even attempt to launch a real revolution of gay liberation in Karachi is to tilt at windmills.

The most successful gay relationships in Karachi are quiet and heavily compromised. They are almost never the most important relationship for either partner; the family occupies that position. But deep affections do develop, though the long-term outcome is almost always a breakup, triggered by differences in family circumstances or demands. Human beings do tend to develop emotional bonds; in Pakistan these bonds either result in tragedy or unacceptable (to a Westernized sensibility) compromises to steal private moments of tenderness or sexual release. To the gay Pakistani, this is simply another of life's compromises.

MEETING PEOPLE

Pakistan is a male-dominated and very homo-social society. In Karachi, men congregate in parks, by the beach, and on street corners. Contact is made in familiar ways: small talk, determination of mutual interest, and the availability of privacy.

During commute hours, most intersections are crowded with young men waiting for buses or open to an invitation. A man drives by in a car and makes eye contact with another man on the lookout, standing separate from the crowd on a street corner. He is offered a ride and gets in. There is a quick pass and (if a private place is available) sex. There is no expectation of a relationship, though relationships between individuals based on continuing periodic sexual episodes are common.

SEXUAL PRACTICES

Sexual activity includes fellatio, anal sex, kissing, and frottage. This author heard of no instance of sadomasochism or other physically brutal forms of lovemaking. Sexual activity is generally perceived as requiring tenderness, passion, good humor, and gracious permissiveness rather than harsh dominance.

In anal intercourse, the insertor tends to be older, the "man," while the insertee tends to be younger, or an available "queen" or masseur. In some encounters, kissing is unacceptable. In yet other encounters a boy will willingly offer himself for anal penetration, but shyly refuse to allow the insertor to see or stimulate his genitals or to kiss him.

In some cases, the passive partner finds anal intercourse (acting as a "woman") more acceptable than fellating the man. (The derisive word *gandu* refers to the insertee in anal sex.) This is in part due to the special significance of rules of cleanliness that are part of the Muslim tradition; the genitals are "unclean," hence it would be improper to suck or swallow semen or ejaculate. However, this is not a general rule, and well-practiced fellators are readily available. Incidentally, such rules of cleanliness are practiced in relation to eating, as well as in routinely washing the anal area after defecation (rather than simply scraping the area with toilet paper in the Western method).

AVAILABILITY OF SEX

There are two classes of available men that bear special note. These are the *mālišhīs* (masseurs) and the hijras. Along many street corners men sit and wait for customers to massage. Most customers are "legitimate," but it is commonly accepted that (for an additional fee) the masseurs will perform sexual services that include passive anal intercourse.

More interesting is the role of hijras, or hermaphrodites. This community consists of men who dress as women, including transvestites, castrati, and true hermaphrodites. It is a tradition in some communities to invite hijras to sing and dance at happy events, such as a wedding or the birth of a son. Hijras are also available as prostitutes, and it is well accepted that men (generally, unmarried men) may purchase their sexual services.[2]

Note that all sexual releases are of the "pragmatic" variety, which assumes that the male (as a sexual animal) needs release before (or in addition to) marriage. Such needs are frowned upon but accepted. What is totally unacceptable is for these outlets to act as a long-term substitute for the "duty" to bear children, or for a special feeling to develop between two men that precludes marriage and the bearing of children.

Love between men is, in fact, exalted, and tenderness, affection, and deep friendships are not uncommon. Unlike the macho backslap that passes for camaraderie in the West, men frequently hold hands while walking, and it is not uncommon to see men embracing. Poetry and popular song use the male gender as the object of affection. This is generally interpreted as a coy reference to women, but songs that talk of undying friendship between men are part of the repertoire of popular verse. There is a strong element of the Mediterranean pedagogical-Socratic love ideal that is seen as ennobling the soul. The affection of men for each other is generally seen as a good thing, and the fear that men in the West have of intimacy with each other is pointedly absent.

The high stature awarded to love between men is a continuation of a tradition that dates to the Moghul era and the traditions of Islamic mysticism (the "Sufis"). These traditions have been diluted with the Hindu and (in the more recent past) Western influence in Pakistan. As mentioned earlier, notions of male bonding remain strong in most rural communities, including the fierce Pathan tribesmen. (This is the same ethnic group that is settled in Afghanistan and has fought off invaders for generations, including, more recently, the Russian invaders. Alexander the Great was unable to conquer them; so he married a tribeswoman to gain safe passage to the rich lands beyond.)

INDIVIDUAL ACCOMMODATIONS TO FAMILIAL DEMANDS

The bustling metropolis can be literally a "sex bazaar" for those seeking release. Local residents have found pragmatic ways of accommodating family and love. The following four cases reflect experiences reported to the author and are strictly anecdotal:

Case 1

Mohammad C. comes from a lower-middle-class family and lives in a modest apartment with his mother and two younger sisters in a high rise near Karachi University. He went to the Middle East as a manual laborer when he was 21 years old and saved up enough to buy a condominium, a car, and start a small business. Now 30 and financially stable, he is under pressure from his mother to get married soon.

He is fully aware of his attraction to men. He hangs around after work with friends to drink tea and talk, but after he leaves them to drive back home his gaze is drawn inexorably to the young men waiting at bus stops and street corners. While his plans for a wife and family of his own were a source of immense satisfaction, it was these boys who aroused his flesh. Most often, this meant a quick trip to the loo to jerk off, stroke himself empty, and wash up. Somehow, this just was not satisfying. Recently, he had gotten into the habit of picking up Mumtaz, a student at nearby Islamia College. Mumtaz was always waiting for him at the roundabout near the Karachi jail at 9 p.m.

Today, Mumtaz was not there. However, his friend Ašraf—the one with the playful eyes, wide smile, and tight, firm buns—was waiting for the bus. Mohammad pulled over.

"He hopped in, and I think he knew I wasn't looking to give him just a ride. He said he was in no hurry. He lived on the other side of town near Malir, and everyone at home was going to be out. I was already hot, and when he reached down and stroked my hard cock, I just pushed the accelerator down all the way. There was nothing to talk about. He took me to his bedroom (which he shared with his brother) and we started embracing before he had locked the door. He wanted to be kissed and caressed and fucked, and he was not bashful about it. I stroked him, we embraced with much affection—on the bed, on the floor. I fucked him while he jerked off, and then we simply cuddled for a while. I reached home in time for bed. I went back after that to Mumtaz, my 'regular,' and never had sex with Ašraf again. I did, of course, occasionally pick up other boys for variety, but Mumtaz was so sweet, he never minded. We got along so well together."

Mohammad was married to his cousin the following year and is now 35 with two children. He still picks up boys for sex, but, when asked whether he is homosexual, he is amused by the question. Yes, he says, he loves men. But he is not one for names and labels. He has a good relationship with his wife, but saves his love for his various lovers and occasional affairs. Mumtaz and he have broken up. No, he and his wife do not have recreational sex, but will start up again (unnatural though it is for him) when they are ready for a third child. He is happy with his life and the balance he has achieved.

Case 2

Tariq is gay. He has lived in London for several years and has had at least two major love affairs. He cheerfully calls himself a "slut" and grumbles that he had to come back to Karachi because his father (a wealthy industrialist) threatened to cut off his allowance since he had dropped out of school. Tariq is 23 and beautiful, with punk-cut wavy hair, a playful smile, and large sensuous eyes. His parents complain that he is irresponsible, and he says they are right. He is gay and feels very trapped in Karachi. His only recreational sex is with the family servants, whom he seduced shortly after his return. There are two servants he has seduced: one is a young Pathan boy who works in the garden, and the other is an older man who is the chauffeur. Both are quite willing to satisfy his needs (and he "tips" them generously for fucking him on a regular basis), but are concerned for their jobs. His parents sense that the servants are losing respect for him, and his decadence frightens them. He needs to get married!

He cannot really disagree with them, but is thoroughly frightened at the prospect. He has been to bed with two women, a disaster each time. While he was able to perform sexually on one of these instances, he finds satisfaction only with men. Then, he functions as insertee, and likes, as he put it, "to feel a man all the way inside me." Marriage to a woman is alien to his sensibilities and profoundly unnatural for him. He is trapped, though, and has little choice but to play along and hope for an exit. His mother is busy scouting for eligible girls, and he is just as busy finding faults with every prospective candidate.

Case 3

Shah was visiting Karachi to see his family. He is a student in the Boston area and a regular fixture at gay bars in Copley Square. In Karachi he felt trapped; as he put it, "being with my family was starting to get on my nerves, and the cute boys hanging around street corners and cruising me when I drove by gave me a perpetual erection." He decided to take matters into his own hands. Here is his story:

"I took the family car for a spin. The roundabout near Clifton was almost empty. I cruised a guy standing on the road and stopped to give him a lift. Our eyes met and my spine tingled. He got into the car and immediately put his hand on my leg, then started stroking my crotch. No preliminaries, just a direct look and a soft stroke. The only question left was, where would we go? He had by now freed my swollen cock, which was erect in his hands. I was groping his crotch while trying to drive, at the same time trying to provide his hand cover by placing my jacket on my lap. We were both hot. We had no place to go the first time . . . I really was poorly prepared! As I drove in circles, he bent over and started sucking me . . . I was freaking out, but his soft lips and warm mouth were tantalizing . . . I drove out to a remote area and just drove in circles, literally, till I came! It was just too much, but what a memory! We met again, and this time we went to bed and had a proper session of affectionate lovemaking. He became my boyfriend for the rest of my visit, which passed very well indeed!"

Case 4

Sex in public places, always a dangerous proposition, is sometimes necessary because of circumstances. Hamīd-ud-Dīn comes from a large lower-class family and has no privacy at home. He really does not concern himself with feelings of guilt or a desire to understand his needs; he simply knows that he likes sex with men and that the only feasible place to make contact is in public places.

He has used friends' houses a couple of times, but generally has to accommodate his needs on the street. He reports that this is easy. Eye contact in public places at dusk, where men congregate just after the evening prayers, generally leads to readily available sex.

"I was walking slowly in the park. It was getting dark. I was dressed in a well-ironed and loose *šalwar kamīz* [loose pyjama-like native dress] and the gentle sway of my hips was designed to coordinate with my open smile. I looked available! Occasionally, I would reach down and play with my genitals, as though scratching my balls. An older guy cruised me, then motioned me towards the bushes. I was horny. Why not!

"As soon as we reached a dark spot near a clump of bushes, he silently stroked me, and I loosened my shalwar. For the next several minutes he gave me a slow and sweet blow job. Then he left, after we had exchanged a long and caring smile. He stroked my cheek gently with his hand and then disappeared."

In these situations, and in others recounted to me, the notion of an exclusive relationship rarely came up. Though multiple sexual contacts with the same man may have been involved (rather than one-night stands) in the episodes related, the satisfaction did not extend beyond the sexual, despite desires that did.

PROGNOSIS

Karachi is a large and relatively (by Pakistan standards) Westernized city. If there is to be any "gay liberation" movement of any kind, its genesis will be in this urban center. Gay men who have lived abroad and returned to their families have already started to influence the rigid rules to some limited degree. In some instances men have been bold enough to live away from their families. Some men have resisted marriage, or openly nurture quiet relationships with other men within the context of a marriage. Almost always, these men must come from families in upper income brackets; their class of peers also include men who have premarital sex with women, and men and women who have extramarital relationships. This upper crust operates, as do upper classes everywhere, in a relatively "amoral" environment where personal desires are neither justified nor condemned by moral strictures.

The great protector of public morality, the middle class, continues to be frighteningly dominated by rules and restrictions, aided by interpretations of religion that are intended to provide the theoretical basis for shackles on behavior. The return to domination by religious doctrine (sometimes called "Islamic fundamentalism") spells trouble for freedom and certainly limits the ability of men to be sexual. Police have been known to raid public places and scapegoat victims at random.

There is some reason to hope that, in the coming decades as the world draws closer, gay life in Karachi may yet develop in the inhospitable soil there.

REFERENCES

1. Murray, Stephen O. (1987). *Male Homosexuality in Central and South America* (Gai Saber Monograph 5). New York: Gay Academic Union.

2. Nanda, Serena (1989). *Neither Man Nor Woman: The Hijras of India*. Belmont, CA: Wadsworth.

Testimonies from the Holy Land: Israeli and Palestinian Men Talk About Their Sexual Encounters

Jehoeda Sofer

INTRODUCTION

The gay tourist to Israel will probably go to the cruising areas of the Independence Parks of Jerusalem and Tel-Aviv or may visit the two and a half gay bars and discos. There he will meet young Israelis who identify themselves as gays. But these places are not more than small enclaves in a basically Oriental country.

About 5 million people live in Israel and the territories occupied in 1967. Since then many Israelis have established relations with inhabitants of the Occupied Territories, including sexual ones. About 1.2 million Palestinians live in the Occupied Territories, and about 0.7 million inside pre-1967 Israel. The number of Jews hailing from Islamic countries of the Middle East and North Africa is about 1.7 million (of which 0.9 million were born in Israel). Moreover, the Balkan Jews (mainly from Bulgaria and Romania) are not really Western, definitely not in their sexual behavior. Israelis coming from Europe and America and their descendants (*Aškenazim*) make up hardly 30% of the total population. These various groups lived and largely still live in segregated cities and neighborhoods.

But the state institutions—army, schools, TV—try their best to westernize the second generation, to cut the Orientals from their roots. This affects their attitude toward women and sexuality as well. Whereas Greek and Arab men may walk on the street hand in hand, kiss and hug each other in public, in Israel it is automatically associated with homosexuality.

The majority of Israelis who engage in sex between males do

not consider themselves as homosexual. They have a great number of meeting places. Between 1970 and 1974 I interviewed hundreds of men in different places in Israel and the Occupied Territories. Here I present a selection of these interviews reflecting the way of thinking and the sexual behavior of most Israelis and Palestinians.

Yitsḥaq

Yitsḥaq was born in ʿIrāq. At twelve he had sex with an older uncle; later he was regularly fucked by men. He started going to coffee shops where he was picked up by men who fucked him. In 1950, when he was 16, his family migrated to Israel, where they, together with other ʿIrāqis, were allotted the Arab village of Hiria (the Palestinian inhabitants left or were made to leave in 1948). Yitsḥaq worked as a dressmaker. Later he moved with his family to Ramat-Gan, a largely ʿIrāqī suburb of Tel-Aviv.

In 1971 he decided to travel to Europe: "I had been looking forward to this trip for several years, and I had worked hard to save money. I had heard from many people about the wonderful possibilities for sex in cities like Paris and Berlin. I started in Amsterdam. During the day I was approached by several men on the street. Although some of them looked very masculine, they all had something soft, something feminine about them, so I did not go with them. On the first night I went to a bar. There were hundreds of men. It was exciting, since I had never seen so many homosexuals in one place. But I was very confused, because I could not distinguish 'men' from 'women' (meaning 'fuckers' and 'fuckees'). Again, there were men who were tall and looked very masculine, but they all had something non-manly, something soft. No one was like the men I used to go with in Israel.

"The second night I went to the same place. I saw a man whom I knew from the cruising park of Ramat-Gan. For five years he had lived in Amsterdam. Since I felt helpless, I asked him how he distinguished men from women. He started laughing and said it did not matter so much here. He said that most of them did both fuck and get fucked. For the next three nights I went back alone to my hotel room. The fourth night I settled for someone, who looked masculine. He didn't fuck me at once: we kissed and played for a long time. Although it was new to me, I liked it; in Israel most men did not do such things. He fucked me a long time without having an orgasm. He came while masturbating. In Europe I have seen many things, and I have learned many things. There is one thing you don't find there: There are no real men!"

Ramat-Gan, April 1974

Yosef

Yosef immigrated to Israel from ʿIrāq at the beginning of the fifties. Along with his daily work as a clerk in Tel-Aviv, Yosef worked as a singer of Arabic music, mainly classical ʿIrāqī music and interpretations of Umm Kulṯum's songs. He was rather popular among ʿIrāqī Jews and Palestinians. He often went to the cruising park of Ramat-Gan. Most regulars had a female name, mainly in order to hide their real name. Yosef could not hide his real identity because he was well known; posters announcing his performances carried his photograph.

Yosef told me several stories about his experiences with Palestinians and ʿIrāqī Jews. Often young men would wait until the end of the show and offer to fuck him. Yosef took only stallions. He would never go a second time with somebody who had shown affection or fussed around instead of doing a good fuck, or whose cock was not big enough.

In Palestinian villages, where he had to stay overnight the organizers prepared a room or a whole house. In one village the organizer was a young married man, who sent his wife to her parents for the night. In such cases it happened that Yosef had to enjoy and satisfy several men, sometimes twelve or fourteen. On such nights, Yosef sang and danced, and the men clapped hands. When he felt that the atmosphere was right, he went to the room put aside. Men entered in order to fuck him, one by one. It never happened that two came at the same time. Because he was respected as a good singer, he felt he had the power to reject someone and to decide the order. Some he invited to stay and have a second go.

The whole village knew the day after who was among the visitors; they were very proud to present him as a friend. Yosef says he was ridiculed only once, by kids. When this happened, the older men told the kids to shut up.

Ramat-Gan, April 1974

Mošē

The Barzilai Park, not far from the Tel-Aviv Central Station was known as 'the small park' (in comparison with Independence Park). Most sexual encounters took place in one of the dark places in the vicinity of the park. Having sex with the same man a second or third time was almost always a question of incident. When there were no 'interesting' men in the surrounding, the 'girls' (hebr. *zonot*, literally whores) would chat, but as soon as a man would appear, the group would split up. Those who were interested in the guy would leave and try to approach him.

Mošē, an Oriental Jew, rather masculine and hairy, told me about an encounter he had had there: "I met Ibrāhīm in the park. We went to a dark courtyard nearby and talked. This was strange to me. Usually, one walked ahead, and the other followed several meters behind, all in order not to give the image of having to do with each other. I never took a man I met in this place to my apartment. We walked to that courtyard not only together, but Ibrāhīm started a conversation. He was married with a son, he told me. He was Christian and lived in Šfarʿam, a big Palestinian town. Once a month he is in Tel-Aviv on business (making orders for his building materials shop).

"I felt that this was going to be different from the usual sexual contact I have had with Palestinians or Oriental Jews. In that courtyard, Ibrāhīm took the initiative. He helped me to take off my shirt. Normally men told me to do that or fucked me half dressed. Usually sex took only some minutes: I was fucked, while bending over. This time it was different. Although there were no kisses, we hugged. He fucked from forward, looking to my face. It took more than twenty minutes. For the first time in my life I had an encounter with an Oriental man, holding back orgasm as long as possible. At the end he asked me to come to his shop in

Šfarʿam. I gave him my telephone number—probably the first time I gave it to a man I met in the 'small park.'

"When I visited him in his home town, he introduced me to his family as a friend coming from the big city, and from a higher class (Jews are always seen as in a higher position). He asked his wife to take the son and to go to her parents, who lived several houses further. She did. He said she had no reason to 'suspect' anything as he was a good husband. He also said the villagers will never suspect for two reasons: he has a son, and I looked too masculine. Indeed, the next time I came to Šfarʿam people approached me as a man of respect and as a friend of Ibrāhīm, not as a fuckee. Ibrāhīm came and stayed several times in my apartment. We have had contact for five years."

Tel-Aviv, August 1978

Edi

Edi, dark-blond, Aškenazi, lives in the richer neighborhood of North Tel-Aviv. He is very effeminate, and likes only to be fucked, preferably by Arabs, Oriental Jews, or other working class men. After the occupation of the West Bank in 1967, he went once or twice a month to Jerusalem, where he approached Palestinian men on the streets, alleys, coffeeshops, etc. He never went to cruising places in the city, as he wanted to have sex with 'real' men.

Every now and then Edi stayed in the Old City overnight. Once he was put together in the same room with four men from Hebron. They all fucked him several times that night. One said: "If the Arabs would have had war with the Israelis using cocks, we would have defeated them easily. The Israeli are a bunch of feminine males who want and should be fucked by the Arabs. Israelis have no self respect, they let themselves and their females be fucked." He also said: "An Arab man will never let himself be fucked." Edi says: "That was the first time I realized sex has a political connotation."

Tel-Aviv, February 1970

Haim

Haim, a South-American Jew, lived for several years in Europe and Israel. He reported to me: "I know that Palestinians are attracted to me because I'm feminine, small, fragile, and blond. I used to go to the cruising area of Independence Park in Jerusalem. One night I saw a group of three men, the youngest extremely beautiful. I approached them and I realized they were Palestinians. We started talking. After a while I made it clear that I would like to have sex with the youngest one. They said they all wanted to fuck me, which I refused outright. I went away.

"After a few minutes I was approached by the young man. He invited me to come with him. He took me to the No Man's Land not far from the Jaffa Gate (this is the area between West and East Jerusalem—No Man's Land until 1967, un-built-up for some years longer). After a few minutes I realized that the other two had followed us. It was an empty area and I could not do much. I was afraid to refuse. I made it clear that in this case I wanted the youngest man to fuck me first, but the older one said that this was not normal: he had the right to be the first and that he was 'a better fucker' and that I would enjoy that more than with the others, as they were younger. I did not agree, but I soon realized that there was no choice. I was scared to death. So they did it, first the oldest, then the one in the middle, the youngest was last. Then the oldest said he wanted to fuck me again. Probably he wanted to show how masculine he was. After fucking me the second time, they left."

Jerusalem, April 1970

David

David, an Egyptian Jew: "I only go to the 'small park' in Tel-Aviv. There, I once met an Arab, a construction worker, from a village in the Galilea. He lived in Givataim, a suburb of Tel-Aviv, in a tiny, neglected room, with nothing in it but a bed, where he took me. It was clear that he was going to fuck me. He did, but he could not keep a hard-on. It took him a long time to have orgasm, something rather unusual. The experience I have with Arab males is that they come very quickly. So, after a while I got tired and I wanted to stop with the whole thing. He could not come while fucking me. He directed me to suck him off, but still he did not come. I then decided to put a finger into his ass hole, and he came almost immediately. He was very insulted and angry and started telling me that I should not put my finger into his ass. Then I apologized. I said I didn't intend to do that, that it was a stupid thing to do, also telling him how masculine and manly he was. Telling him how much I enjoyed being fucked by such a real man. That I prefer to go with Arab men, like him, because they were good fuckers and real men. His anger then tempered. He said that I should never assume that he would let anybody fuck him. I am however sure that he would have liked very much to get fucked, but will probably never admit it. He also said he normally fucks only women. However, he was seen regularly in that park."

Tel-Aviv, June 1973

Ša'ūl

Ša'ūl, an ʿIraqī Jew from Ramat-Gan, big, masculine, well hung, and very popular among males who wanted to get fucked, often seen with his wife and two children, frequents cruising place. Although he says he is not 'like that' he socializes with 'men like that' in the parks. He goes only with fair, effeminate men, whom he addresses in the feminine (Hebrew distinguishes genders throughout). Ša'ūl said being sucked off was O.K., but fucking was much more enjoyable. He said he would be furious if such a 'woman' would achieve an orgasm in his presence, let alone if it would happen before he himself would achieve an orgasm. He would slap 'her' in the face. He would never touch the genitals of the 'woman' he fucked. He was 'not like that' because he was married with two boys, and would never let anybody fuck him.

Ramat-Gan, May 1974

Eli

Eli, non-masculine, non-feminine Aškenazi from North Tel-Aviv: "I once met a Moroccan Jew in the 'small park' of Tel-Aviv. He took me to his home and fucked me. His wife was at that time pregnant, and was hospitalized in order to save the child. She had had two miscarriages before. In fact, he said, he went to the 'small park' in order to have sex with a female prostitute. He asked a female prostitute to accompany him to his home, but then he realized she would charge him a fortune. She said that if he is such a cheap man, he should go and do it in the arsehole of one of the males walking around. Without sex for three weeks he was really horny. Since two Moroccan friends had told him that they had fucked males he decided to try it too.

"He treated me lovingly and caringly. Although I believe that I was his first man, he did it in a very natural way. I did feel that he enjoyed fucking a man. He asked me at the end if I wanted to meet him again. We did it several times. I always knew that the relationship would end as soon as his wife came out of the hospital.

"A year later I met him again in the 'small park.' His wife was again pregnant."

Tel-Aviv, March 1974

Eliezer

"I saw the man sitting with three other men in a coffee shop in Acre. They watched me, and I watched back. Then I went away. After five minutes I passed by that coffee shop again. They were still sitting there. I kept walking, and I noticed that one of them, thirtyish, followed me. I walked and climbed the city wall I knew to be a quiet place. He asked if I was looking for drugs. I said no, but that I would no doubt enjoy it if he would fuck me. He said he was not into it, but if I was willing to pay him 75 Israeli pounds, he would not mind doing it. I then started laughing, saying that there are so many men who would die to fuck me for free, and that I saw no reason why I should pay. I walked away slowly. He then called me and said he would do it for 50 Is£. A few seconds later he came down to 25 İs£. I refused again. He fucked me. While he was fucking me two Arab boys walked along, but did as if they saw nothing. After he had achieved an orgasm, he said that I should not think that he had enjoyed it, since he is not 'like that,' and demanded compensation. I gave him a package of cigarettes and went away.

"After visiting the old market I walked along the same coffee shop. One of his three friends followed me this time. I climbed the city wall again, went to the same place, and the man followed. He said that if I wanted to get fucked I should pay him 50 İs£, exactly as I did with his friend. I informed him that I had not paid his friend, but he insisted that his friend has shown them the 50 İs£ and the package of cigarettes. 'If you want to fuck me, you can do so. But without any payment,' I said. After a few minutes of argumentation he agreed to fuck me for free."

Acre, June 1970

Šmu'el

Šmu'el, an Aškenazi, lives in Jerusalem, frequents the Jerusalem Independence Park, is attracted to working class males, especially Arabs, and likes to get fucked. He tells: "Walking in the narrow alleys of Old Jerusalem I am often approached by men for sex. Although I am not really effeminate, there is something about my behavior which is recognizable. I have been fucked by quite a few Arabs. Since they are not ashamed to tell each other, many men know about me.

"One day I was talking with a shopkeeper with whom I have had sex before. There was another man in the shop, young, masculine, and very sexy. I addressed him. He introduced himself as Amar. Soon it was clear that we both wanted to have sex. We went to the one-room steam bath, near the Temple Mount. Amar knew the old owner, who didn't have to be told the purpose of our visit. It was after 7 p.m., a time not many clients were expected, so we could feel free to do whatever we wanted. Besides, it was clear to me that the owner would not let somebody in who might take offense.

"Amar fucked me three times in two hours. We hardly talked since my Arabic was weak and he did not speak Hebrew at all. In one of the breaks he said we were expected to tip. It was clear that I had to pay it and the fees. We had tea, and a chat with the owner and two other older men that had come a few minutes earlier. I believe that the two visitors knew what I was doing there. After drinking the tea I decided to leave, and Amar left with me.

"For Old Jerusalem it was late, hardly anybody was around. I wanted to eat something in the only snack bar open. I asked Amar if he wanted to join me. He agreed and told me that I had to pay him 25 pounds, which I refused. But he insisted, saying that he is not 'like that,' that he did not enjoy it at all, that he had to get a compensation, that he needed a whole meal because he has lost much power and blood by coming three times. I have said that we did not agree upon such a payment, but he said we did not have to because it was obvious and a matter of course, that he has been always paid for sex. When I answered that I was not convinced by that, and that he could forget about it, he became angry and threatened me. There was nobody around, and I felt a bit insecure. However I walked in the direction of the Jaffa Gate. He started being louder. I told him that he should not forget that he is an Arab, that under Israeli rule he had no case against a Jew, and that he'd better leave me alone. I never would have dared to go to the police, but it worked. I also knew that he was deeply insulted, as he realized that the fuckee is not powerless, as he assumed.

"Amar kept quiet and agreed to join me at the snack bar. There were five men, who greeted Amar. While eating Amar told the other men that he had fucked me three times in order to humiliate me. The men started laughing at me. I felt very embarrassed and uncomfortable. For a long time I did not dare to walk near that snack bar anymore."

Jerusalem, April 1970

Sven

Sven, a Norwegian, has lived in Israel for three years. He is the type of man many Israelis desire: in his twenties, blond, suntanned, hairless, soft but not feminine. In Norway, where he had sex with men from the age of 17, sex had meant a lot of different techniques.

"In Israel I was extremely attracted to dark men; Palestinian Arabs and Oriental Jews in their late thirties, early forties. At the beginning I was rather confused: most men only wanted to fuck me. After a while I started liking it.

"Once I had sex with a Moroccan Jew, who fucked me in the bushes of Independence Park in Jerusalem. I did not enjoy it. But he probably did. Next time I met him he suggested a repeat performance. I refused. I moved away but he kept following. He insisted that I go with him. Since he wouldn't leave me alone, I retreated. Three or four times the same thing happened. He was probably in love, or something like that. One night he was so desperate, he even offered money. I told him very clearly that he had no chance at all, that I didn't find him attractive enough, that I didn't enjoy having sex with him. I ordered him to leave me alone. I probably hurt him by suggesting that he was not a good fucker. He started screaming and yelling at me, telling me I am not a man, that I didn't deserve to be respected and that I have the honor of a prostitute. He screamed I should leave and never show my face in this park again. I told him to forget it, I had the right to go wherever I wished.

"I don't know exactly what happened, but I found myself lying on the ground; my lips were bleeding, I had a terrible headache, and pain all over my body. People helped me to the taxi-station nearby. For four months I didn't go to Independence Park out of fear."

Jerusalem, April 1971

Dani

Dani, a Yemenite Jew from Petah Tiqwah, had his first sex with men at the age of fourteen. He was fucked and he enjoyed it—never considering the possibility of fucking. He had many sexual encounters with men from his Yemenite neighborhood. He frequented the cruising areas of Tel-Aviv. He and his friends believed that they could enjoy sex only by playing the receptive role. When he could not avoid it, he did fuck, but did not enjoy it.

He wanted a lasting relationship with a clear division of sexual roles. At twenty-five he finally met an Aškenazi teacher at the University, with whom he lived for three years as housewife both in bed and in the kitchen. His friend did not consider himself homosexual and left Dani to marry.

In order to forget, Dani went abroad and lived in Berlin for seven years. In Berlin Dani did well. He had few problems with the differences between the cultures: Already in Israel he had put a lot of energy into trying to adopt an Aškenazi Western lifestyle, thus cutting the bridge with his Yemenite background.

About his experiences in Berlin he says: "In Israel I grew up in an environment where I really believed you had to choose between two options: fuck or get fucked. Other sexual activities like kissing, embracing, etc. occurred, but were less important. These were the ideas I came with to Berlin. That was also how I lived at the beginning.

"In Berlin I started frequenting the bars. For years I did not cruise in parks. That was something that reminded me too much of Israel, where besides parks and public toilets you had no choice.

"I realized that the ideas about sex I had been brought up with were of no use in these bars: here everybody identified himself as homosexual. There were no straight men out to fuck. I understood that no clear separation existed between men who fuck and men who get fucked; that these are not two separate worlds.

"However, I did not really change my sexual behavior and my attitude towards sex with men until I fell in love with a German guy, with whom I had relations for six months. I was so terribly in love with this man, I enjoyed every minute with him. Most of the time he fucked, but from time to time he wanted to get fucked; so I did. At first it was because I feared I would lose him if I didn't satisfy his sexual needs. Later I realized that I enjoyed doing it with the man I loved. To my surprise it was not difficult to get an erection when I had to fuck him. Before that I used to lose my erection just at the thought of having to fuck someone.

"I also learned to appreciate other sexual techniques. Although I still prefer being fucked, I also appreciate and enjoy other forms of sex. Now, after seven years in Berlin, I do not believe, and cannot even understand how I ever believed, that if you fuck you may not get fucked and vice versa.

Berlin, September 1981

Samīr

It was early in the afternoon, and only a few people were in Tel-Aviv's Independence Park. When I entered the tearoom, Samīr followed me. Seeing my interest, he offered sex for money: five shekel for a blow job, ten for fucking. I refused.

A short while later I was talking with a friend. We called Samīr over. While chatting, again and again he offered sex for payment. Whenever someone entered the toilets, Samīr went after him, but came back if it did not work.

Samīr, 32, is an Israeli Palestinian, born and raised in Jaffa, married with three children (a fourth son died recently). He visits the park two to three times a week, and does sex with men only for money, and he plays the penetrating role only. Later he admitted that he would fuck boys or young, blond and beautiful men without payment.

While talking, Samīr saw a young man. He became excited, and chased the guy for more than 20 minutes. "With such a beautiful boy I will agree to have sex without payment, if he insists or cannot pay," he explained.

In the past he fucked men for free, if they introduced him to women. In fact, he prefers women. When it happened that he is with a man and a woman together, the woman always goes first. With his wife he has sex two or three times a day. He has never fucked a prostitute.

At 17 he had sex for the first time: he fucked a Palestinian boy of 14, Fathi, several times. Today Fathi is married, works as a truck driver, and has no sex with males. Samīr said he recently tried to approach Fathi sexually, but was refused. "For me he remains a fuckee. It doesn't matter that he's married and doesn't do it any more," said Samīr. Fathi was his only Palestinian sex partner. Today he would fuck Arabs if they wanted to—not only boys but also young men. "But young Palestinian men will not let themselves be fucked. Why should they?

"Having sex with males is not tolerated by the Arab community in Jaffa. I feel uncomfortable when I see an Arab man I know in the park. We won't talk to each other, although we both know the purpose of our being there. If we meet in Jaffa, we pretend not to have seen each other in the Tel-Aviv park. Therefore he never goes to the cruising park in Jaffa. He is sure that his wife would leave him if she found out about him. The fact that he satisfies her sexually wouldn't make a difference."

Tel-Aviv, April 1973

Sālim

Sālim, 22 years old, lives in East Jerusalem, and works in a Tel-Aviv restaurant washing dishes. After work, around two o'clock he often goes to Independence Park. There I met him. He told me that he fucks men because it is his only chance to have sex, but that, needless to say, he preferred women.

However, meeting a Palestinian woman for sex before marriage is almost impossible. Jewish women, he says, do not go with Palestinians. Even female Jewish prostitutes discriminate against Arabs: they charge prices Sālim cannot pay, or reject them totally. So, he looks for sexual satisfaction with the men in the parks in Tel-Aviv and West Jerusalem. Mostly he does not ask for payment, but if the man is old or looks rich he does. He is not interested in a lasting relationship with a man, because "I am not a homosexual. I was never fucked, and I will never let anybody fuck me. As soon as I have enough money and get married, I will stop coming here. Men who let themselves get fucked are not men. They have lost their respect. Among Arabs this is a shame for the whole family.

"At school we had a boy, Sālim, whose older brother was known as a 'fucked one.' Although he was a good pupil and excellent in sports, we did not consider Sālim a real man. Sometimes when there was a quarrel in which Sālim was involved, his opponent called him a 'fucked one,' even though no one really thought he was.

"In East Jerusalem I know of another man, whose father was fucked before getting married. When the son first heard of it, he immediately cut off contact with his nearly 60-year-old father. He is now working in Kuwait. We naturally never talked about the subject in his presence, but in conversations he was sometimes referred to as 'Ibn al manyak,' i.e., son of the fucked one.

Tel-Aviv, May 1974

Arab Men in Paris

Dominique Robert

Paris, *Gare du Nord*, Saturday afternoon. Samaḥ is leaning against the fotomat. Samaḥ speaks French with difficulty. He is 32 and comes from Algiers. He works in a car factory and lives in a hostel for men in a working class district north of Paris. His daily routine is travelling to the factory, working, eating in a hurry, sleeping a bit. And the weekend? Loneliness. Sometimes a meeting of chaps around a *couscous* [the 'national' dish of Northwest Africa]. No French friend. Saturday he comes to [the oriental quarter of] Barbès and the *Gare du Nord*. Married? Divorced. His wife in Algeria kept nagging him to take her with him to Paris. He likes "men as much as women. There is no difference."

Nearby stands Pierre, 37, a clerk. "I come around here only once in a while, because there are only Arabs." So far, nothing new. Just the familiar attitudes.

One million four hundred thousand Northwest Africans live in France (816,000 Algerians, 442,000 Moroccans, 193,000 Tunisians); they provide a good part of the unskilled labor in industry and construction. It is worthwhile for the French economy and French companies to employ these workers: they accept low wages and bad working conditions, and few are trade union members.

"You make the man or the woman?" That is the important question, important because honor is at stake: one must see to it that only the sex object is not the normal one, and the sexual role is. Most consider themselves heterosexuals, certainly not as *aṭṭa'i*. The Maġribi term *aṭṭa'i* means 'somebody who gives his arse, somebody who submits.' It is a very humiliating term.[1] It equates the fucked ones to women and their position in society is really low. . . . In a way the position of the *aṭṭa'i* is that of a woman, he is a monstrous whore, who has renounced his sex, his reproductive social function, and The One who rules the order of things: God himself.

The *aṭṭa'i* occupies more or less the place the sodomite used to have in Christian society: a demon, a bringer of evil, somebody who destroys the honor of the whole family, the honor of the family patriarch. Most young *aṭṭa'i* know that their father is prepared to do all he has to do in order to clean his name. . . .

Le Palace, Sunday afternoon. Nahīm, 26, well integrated in the gay scene, works in the body-building studio of a big company. Sporting, French nationality. He sees his family in Marseille only once or twice a year. In order to live the life of a homosexual he had to renounce his roots. An Arab can only accept himself as homosexual, as gay, by being westernized. Even today the languages of Northwest Africa inhibit 'being homosexual' by not providing a positive word for it. And for us (Frenchmen)—living in a country with a strong secular tradition—it is much easier to undo the wrongs of religion than for the Arabs for whom religion is still part of everyday life.

Bar Central, Murad, 32, Berber, married. His wife lives in Algeria; he lives with a French friend. Employed as a printer. Murad pays a lot of attention to his appearance: suit, tie, etc. . . . He talks negatively about hustlers and all who are recognizable as homosexuals. That is his way to mark himself off, to come to terms with a world that leaves no respectable place for a homosexual.

Yamin, 40, Algerian, construction worker, 2,800 Francs monthly, a miserable room in Boulevard de la Chapelle for 400 Francs. Yamin makes ends meet by selling pleasure. His clients? Mostly young folks. Why are they willing to pay? "I have no difficulties finding them." On his bed, porno magazines, all with hairy men. His wife? "In Algeria." Women here? "Seldom." What does he know about the gay scene in Paris? "No idea? Where? What?" Where does he cruise? Cinemas, sometimes the embankment of the canal St. Martin.

Among those cruising in the open-air in the evening, Arabs play an important part. This exposes them to police harassment, attacks by hooligans and crime: recently a Northwest African was murdered near the canal St. Martin.

The rate of unemployment among the immigrants is about 50% higher than the average. When the problems of unemployment are added to those of uprootedness and racism, it is understandable that some end up ignoring certain values. But that is not the full story. Here is another aspect: Aḥmed, a young hustler in the *La Nuit* bar, near Pigalle, explains to me that he does it "for the money" and since he invests [no feelings and gets] no real pleasure, he is no *ḥassās*. . . .

Rašīd, 28, married in Tunisia, unskilled laborer in a car factory, 4,200 FF monthly, lives with his brother. He works the whole week and sleeps the weekend. Saturday he sleeps very long, then breakfast, a nap, supper, TV, and sleep again. But from 5 to 7 in the afternoon he "takes a walk." If Rašīd were better integrated into French society he would sit on the sling and practice fist fucking . . . (?) He does not like to fuck and he says that most of his contacts are disappointing, because his strong body evokes the prejudice of the 'Arab super stallion.'

For Rašīd and those like him the French gay scene is a closed world. Although his short hair, his broad shoulders, and his magnificent moustache could serve as the magical 'Open sesame!' to many places, he lacks the usual marks. Racism normally is not of the aggressive and insulting kind, but cold and polite, an ill-concealed unease, a general mistrust: "Ah, monsieur, I am sorry, this establishment is a private club, you need a membership card." Our fine society hides true feelings behind good manners and conventions as rigid as they are hypocritical.

The Arab culture is deeply and strongly hostile to homosexuals; it offers no positive image, no moral support for someone perceiving himself as homosexual. Certain European translators and compilers affirm that the old oriental poetry offers nice examples for the interested reader—but mostly they forget to mention that these texts are about love of boys, in which the relation of age and the relation of power is similar to the prevailing type of heterosexual couple. The only form of homosexuality understandable to orientals preserves the man-woman polarity in the form of man-youth (hard-soft, strong-weak, penetrating-yielding). The man preserves his privilege—a pedestal from which he deigns to regard the beauty of virgins and the childish grace of boys. The masculine body is never treated as desirable.

ʿAlī, 36, a driver, always in suit and tie, really only likes old men. He cruises seldom, since he has his regular contacts. He does not ask for money: "One does not have to pay for pleasure!" ʿAlī always has a good time, he knows everybody and he helps where help is needed: finding an apartment, a car, a lover, a fridge . . . all with a smile. "I love only the old, I always did." ʿAlī is confronted with two taboos: homosexuality and gerontophilia. ʿAlī knows that many cannot understand him.

Aḥmad, 27, a student from Algeria, offers this analysis: "The western view of Arab homosexuality is distorted by the stereotype of the masculine buggerer and the willing youth. The truly homosexual desire has been obscured by two major factors: Islām and colonialism. When you study the Arab literature—although censored, fumbled with, finally castrated—you will find that homosexual writers were treated positively during the Baghdad caliphate . . . and in Muslim Spain. We must dig out these sources, like *The Thousand and One Nights* whose erotic and philosophical significance is seriously underestimated. Modern literature also has difficulties treating the subject, M. Choukri for example."

On the subject of Arabs and the gay scene he says: "First there should be no rejection. Second, many prefer anonymous, ambiguous places to bars clearly defined as homosexual and thus conflicting with the inherited idea of virility."

NOTE

1. The following sentence of D. Robert's article is wrong. He writes: "To like male bodies means to become a woman of sorts, to stop being a man" («Avoir le goût des corps d'hommes implique donc l'identification à la femme et par conséquent renonciation à la masculinité.»). This is only true for those who like to get fucked—liking male bodies, i.e., to look at them, to touch them, to fuck them is perfectly masculine and perfectly all right. [a.s.]

Sexual Meetings of East and West: Western Tourism and Muslim Immigrant Communities

Arno Schmitt

CONTACT WITHOUT QUALITATIVE CHANGE

As Gianni de Martino observes tourists are not the only men in the East who run after boys and youth. There were always men willing to pay boys and fuck them. And even today there are probably more Arab men coming from the oil-rich states to Tunis and Cairo for that than Europeans and Americans.

It was always possible to fuck other males. True, these were normally boys or transvestites, who had to be compensated. But there were some older men who payed for getting fucked, and some young men who just did it.

The presence of western men (whether tourists, businessmen, technical advisors, settlers, or soldiers) brings only quantitative change. Boys and prostitutes get less frequented, and some tourists drive prices up. This is reinforced by female tourists; they offer an even more acceptable outlet for virile power and some make generous gifts.

These contacts are not only interesting on an individual level, but reflect and influence the relations between Westerners and Easterners in general. Whereas the fucking of Muslim boys by Westerners is seen as exploiting the Third World and thus causing resentment, fucking Westerners, whether male or female, is seen as a well deserved revenge for suffered injustice and as an expression of physical and moral superiority over a decaying West.

This compensatory aspect becomes very clear in a Palestinian saying of his fucking an Israeli soldier: "I fucked the Israeli army!" The fuckee is despised and humiliated. Of course this feeling cannot always be shown; if you want to live in someone's apartment, or if you want to be invited to Europe, you have to show affection, not scorn.

And sometimes there will be true affection, especially when the European takes the role of the woman, not only in bed, but accepts 'his man' as protector, as the only channel to the unfamiliar world, allowing 'the husband' to show his acquisition around.

The immigrant communities in Europe present the same picture: many (bisexual) fuckers; some children/youth whose role depends on pay; greater accessibility of (European) women.

In most countries two phases of Muslim communities can be discerned: In the sixties there were mainly single migrant workers, coming for three or four years, then being replaced by fresh compatriots.

But some did not return, some brought their wives to the temporary exile. Children arrived. The transit became permanent. In the mid-seventies the influx was stopped. Instead of single men (or men with their wives 1,000 miles away) between 20 and 30, we now find an almost normal population: half female, half male, many children, some old people.

The best books on our subject are too old to treat the second phase; they are both in French: *Trois Milliards de Pervers* by a gay Frenchman[1] and *La plus haute des solitudes* by a Moroccan, Tahar Ben Jelloun.[2]

In the first period many men in the prime of life were looking for a sexual outlet, many preferring men because they were a) cheaper than prostitutes, b) less demanding than women (less courting necessary), and c) many 'homosexuals' are quite happy with a quick fuck.

Now the situation is more normal. There are still some unmarried men; but knowing the language better than their predecessors twenty years ago, and having adapted somewhat to the culture of the "host" country, it is easier for them to approach girls and women. So today most men with Muslim background still looking for men as sex objects/partners do prefer men—whether they know it themselves or not.

INDIVIDUAL ETHNO-CLIMBERS/ INDIVIDUAL ACCULTURATION

Whereas most sexual contact between Westerners and Muslims followed the Eastern pattern of 'man/non-man,' some Easterners adopted the modern role of 'homosexual/gay.' This happened, for example, in Algiers during the French rule. Some natives, not wanting to play the role of stallions for the French *pédés* any more, nor finding the life of a traditional Algerian transvestite attractive, mingled with the settler 'homosexuals': they perfected their command of French, adopted French dress, tried to live in settler quarters—either moving in with a *colon* or on their own: they became French. So normal Algerians could go on thinking of Algerians as 'men' and of homosexuals as French.

The situation was similar in cities like Alexandria, Cairo, Bagdad, Tunis, Jerusalem, Jaffa/Tel Aviv. . . . And it happens today in Europe among the relatively 'white' Muslims. In Berlin, for example, some Turks who discover that they prefer men and like to mingle with gays, adopt a German or (if they are too dark) an Italian or half-blood identity—leaving the parental home, either to move in with a friend or to live on their own. It remains to be seen how many of them will eventually (at 35 plus) marry and become—albeit modern—Turks again.

If parents detect this unwelcome westernization of their boy, they may try to prevent the worst by sending him 'back' to live with his grandparents or with his uncles, doing his military service and thus becoming a man after all.[3]

INDIVIDUAL SOCIAL CLIMBERS

There is an interesting parallel to this in upwardly mobile native (i.e., European) working class men: they either adopt middle class values and live in gay style or live their homosexuality rather as the 'bisexuality' accepted in their milieu. Both Muslim and European working class cultures accept homosexual sex as one form of sex among others, but reject homosexuals. European middle class culture, on the other hand, tries (tried) to suppress homosexual sex, but leaves room for a small subculture of homosexuals.

EFFECT OF EUROPEAN GAYS ON 'MUSLIM' PERCEPTION

For Arabs and Turks the striking feature about gays is not the existence of men having sex with men, but their openness, the relative naturalness and their 'admitting it' without shame. In Muslim culture honor is not lost by doing something but by being seen doing it, by not at least denying it. (All right, it is obvious, but these shameless people do not even attempt to deny it.)

This can be both confusing and reassuring; confusing as long as you accept a certain superiority of the West, reassuring when you find that in some respect you are superior. The former attitude is common among the modernizing secularizing Muslims, the latter among those looking for identity and support in a new interpretation of Islām.

ADMONITION I

The characteristic pattern of a culture should not be used to reduce persons (sex partners) to perfect models of this pattern, but as the background against which everybody 'belonging' to that culture has to act, i.e., as the base on which each individual has to create his/her own life.

The fact that the culture of the central lands of Islām is different should be used neither to restrict the individual (i.e., to enforce an 'ethno protection zone'), nor as the starting point from which the Muslim has to be 'civilized' in order to become a full fledged human being—i.e., a European by behavior, but should be acknowledged as a precondition for mutual understanding, for learning from each other, learning about one's own cultural conditioning, one's own blind spots, one's own implicit unconscious judgements, and as a base for learning about the culture of one's partner.

ADMONITION II

Please note that this book is mostly concerned with Muslim culture, not with Muslim religion. Indeed it can be argued that the cultural unity between the northern and southern Mediterranean is greater than the common traits between Muslim Egypt and Muslim Indonesia or Muslim Nigeria.

NOTES

1. *Les Arabes et nous* in the magazine *recherches* mars 1973 *Trois milliards des perverse, Grand Encyclopédie des Homosexualité*, Paris.
2. PhD 1975, published 1977: Paris, de Seuil.
3. Finally there are quite a few 'homosexuals' moving to Europe because they find the life in their home country unbearable—either economically, politically, or sexually. Some of them have difficulties with the predominant idea of 'no-fixed-roles'; they think they have to adapt and allow the partner to fuck them after having fucked him or conversely try to perform on the man who fucked them before. Many fail.

Sodomy in the Law of Muslim States

Jehoeda Sofer

THE PENAL CODE

The constitution of all Arab states except Lebanon declares Islām to be the state religion,[1] and the Law of Islām, the *šarīʿa*, to be a main source of state law.[2] But most of these states have or had a penal code strongly influenced by West European law.

The legal and judicial systems of the Arab states, and of Turkey, Irān, and Afġanistān underwent enormous changes during the last 100 years. In some cases, Islāmic law has been discarded in all areas but the law of personal status and family relations; others reformed the Islāmic law itself or integrated parts of the *šarīʿa* into secular law.

Thus, today, the criminal justice systems in the states of the geographical 'core of Islām' may be broadly divided into three groups:

1. states that regard the *šarīʿa* as the law and still apply it wherever possible;
2. states that have abandoned the *šarīʿa* and have substituted secular law; and
3. states with a mixed system, either by having two judicial systems or by incorporating religious law into the secular law.

ISLĀMIC LAW

Islāmic and Western Law are quite different. The latter is thought to be of human, social origin; it responds, more or less quickly and effectively, to the changing patterns of social and economic life. The former constitutes divine law, which is, in theory, immutable—Muslim society is required to adapt to it, and not the other way around.

In classical Islām, there is no separation between the sacred and the secular. The law not only specifically sets forth man's relationship with God, but also the proper organisation of the (religious) community. Crime and sin both fall within the scope of the *šarīʿa*.

Pursuant to the penal law, five acts are 'crimes against God': fornication (*zinā*), slander of fornication (*qadf*), drinking of wine (*šurb al-ḥamr*), theft (*sariqa*), and road robbery (*qaṭʿ aṭ-ṭarīq*). Most Islāmic jurists parallel sodomy (*liwāṭ*) with fornication, albeit often with a different punishment.

In the Qur'ān, sodomy is strongly condemned in a number of verses relating to Lot and his people, telling more or less the Biblical story of Sodom and Gomora (Genesis XIX, 1-23).[3] There is, however, no clear punishment prescribed. This is made good by sayings attributed to the Prophet (*ḥadīṯ*, pl. *aḥadīṯ*). He is said to have declared that both the active and the passive should be stoned; in another *ḥadīṯ* the punishment varies: stoning for a man, who has had coition within a valid marriage or within a legal concubinage (such a man is called *muḥṣan*), but 'only' 100 strokes (and banishment for a year) for a bachelor. Sometimes a distinction is made between 'active' and 'passive,' free and slave, and between adult and minor.

The rules of penal procedure are extremely strict. Only oral testimony by eye witnesses is admitted. Four trustworthy Muslim men must testify that they have seen "the key entering the key hole" or the culprit must confess four times. Since there is a severe punishment for unproven accusation, the punishment was rarely carried out.

The different approaches of the six most important law doctrines will be discussed in this paper in a country-by-country survey: the Ḥanafi school in the Afġhanistān chapter, the Šafiʿite and the Zaidī schools under the North Yemen heading, the Mālikī together with the new Libyan legislation; Ḥanbalism being the official doctrine in Saʿūdī-ʿArabia, will be presented there; and Imamism (Ǧafarite Šiʿa) in the chapter on Irān.

THE BRITISH INFLUENCE

The Indian Penal Code is one of three codes introduced in the British Empire. A first draft was made between 1834-38. In 1858, the Crown took control from the East Indian Company and two years later, after renewed deliberations in the Legislative Council, the Code became law in India. Later it was used in British-ruled territories of the Middle East—the Colony of Aden, Bahrain, Kuwait, Muscat and Oman, Qaṭar, Somaliland, the Sudan, and the Trucial States (today United Arab Emirates).

Article 377 of the Indian Penal Code punishes sodomy by deportation for 20 years, imprisonment for a term of up to 10 years, or by a fine.[4]

In 1956, this Code was replaced in the British territories of the Persian Gulf by a new Penal Code.[5] Article 171 made sodomy punishable by imprisonment not exceeding 10 years, with or without corporal punishment.

THE FRENCH INFLUENCE

The Code Napoléon makes no distinction between sexual intercourse between members of the same sex on one hand and between males and females on the other. It has been suggested that this was a result of Jean-François-Regis de Cambaceres, the head of the drafting commission, loving males. In fact, it should be seen as springing from the principles of the French Revolution.

An amendment to the Penal Code from 1832 provides that only sexual intercourse with persons under the age of 11 was punishable. In 1863 the age of consent was raised for both sexes to 13 years. The Nazi-controlled regime introduced, in 1942, different ages of consent. Sex with a person of the same sex under the age of 21 was prohibited, while the age of consent for heterosexual sex remained 13. In 1945 it was raised to 15. Only in 1981, the age of consent for homosexual acts was brought into line with this.[6]

The Code Napoléon has had a great influence on legislation in the region—partly via the Italian Code Penal: not only in the states which were ruled by the French, but also in Egypt, Turkey, and Libya.

COUNTRY-BY-COUNTRY SURVEY

Afġanistān

Afġan legislation is inspired by Islāmic law. Article 168 of the Penal Code of 1924 made sodomy punishable by death. In 1925, this was changed to *taʿzīr*: the judge could choose any punishment—even the death penalty (Article 132).[7] This penal code was suspended in 1929 when King Amānullāh, a reformer, was dethroned and the *šarīʿa* was reinstated. For the Ḥanafi majority (there is a substantial Šiʿite minority), this brought no change (as far as sodomy is concerned) because Article 132 enshrines the postclassical Ḥanafi view.

Originally the Ḥanafites stated that sodomy is not fornication and must not be punished in the same way. The judge should impose imprisonment and/or flagellation (cf. Muḥammad ibn al-Husain as-Saibani, one of the founders of the school: *Al-Ğāmiʿ as-Saġīr*).[8] The Ḥanafites followed this interpretation for some 700 years.

Later jurists moved closer to the other Sunni schools. Ibrāhīm al-Ḥalabī (in his *Multaqa al-Abḥūr*[9]) prescribes for sodomy, with males as well as with females, death by stoning if the man is *muḥṣan* and whipping if non-*muḥṣan*. Others simply widened the scope of the judge's power: he cannot only sentence to imprisonment and whipping, but to death as well.[10] The 1925 code followed this line.

In 1973, a new Penal Code was enacted. I was not able to find out if sodomy is mentioned in this code.

Algeria

According to Article 388 of the Penal Code (adopted June 8, 1966) sodomy may be punished with imprisonment from two months to two years and a fine (500-2,000 Alg. dinars). Sodomy upon a male person under 18 years may be punished with imprisonment of up to three years and a fine of up to 10,000 dinars.[11]

On June 19, 1984, a "Code de la Famille" based on Islāmic principles was passed. Sodomy may be punished with imprisonment from two months to two years.[12]

Bahrain

The Indian Penal Code was replaced in 1956 by a new Penal Code. Article 171 made 'unnatural sexual offences' punishable with imprisonment not exceeding 10 years, with or without corporal punishment.[13] This Code remained in force after independence.[14]

Egypt

Egypt attained its judicial independence under the H̱edive Isma'il. In 1883 a Penal Code, a Code of Penal Procedure, and four other Codes were promulgated; they represented extensive adoption of Napoléonic legislation.

The Penal Code of 1904 borrowed from the Sudanese (that is, the Indian) Penal Code and from the Italian Penal Code of 1899.[15] The legislation concerning sexual offences provided only a new age of consent for aggravated rape: it was changed from 12 years to 16.

The code of 1937 (Law № 58; based on the Italian model) brought the same type of change: Article 269 of the Penal Code of 1904 punished indecent acts committed against children under the age of 14; now it is under the age of 21 (in 1883 it was still 12 years). Note that none of these codes distinguishes between boys and girls.[16]

Irān (The Islamic Republic of)

The Penal Code passed in the parliament of the Islāmic Republic of Irān on October 12, 1982 is the classical law of the Imāmīya in the modern form of the code.

In the third chapter of its Second Part the Penal Code deals with sodomy[17] (and lesbian acts[18]). Both the active and the passive sodomite (Article 140) must be put to death in a manner decided by the judge (Article 141) provided the culprit is mature, of sound mind, and free will (Article 142). If an adult sodomizes a minor, the adult will be killed and the boy will be punished at the judge's discretion (*taʿzīr*; Article 143). If both are minors they will be subjected to a punishment decided by the judge (Article 144). A boy will not be punished if raped.

The crime has to be proved by four confessions (Article 145) or four witnesses. If the culprit confesses less than four times, he will be subjected to a lesser punishment decided by the judge (Article 147). Sodomy may also be proved by the testimony of four trustworthy Muslim men who must have seen the act—the testimony of women, Jews, and men of ill repute is not valid (Article 148). Statements made by less than four trustworthy Muslim men are not valid and these 'false' witnesses must be punished for slander (Article 149).

Rubbing of the penis between thighs or buttocks without penetration (*tafhīd*) shall be punished by 100 lashes for each person; but if the 'active' man is non-Muslim and the 'passive' man is Muslim, the non-Muslim will be condemned to death (Article 152). If *tafhīd* is repeated three times and punishment is enforced each time, the punishment for the fourth time would be death (Article 153).

If two men not related by blood are naked under one cover without good reason, both will be punished as the judge deems appropriate (Article 154).

If a male kisses another with lust, he will be punished at the judge's discretion (Article 155).

A person who repents and confesses before his deed is proved by four witnesses may be pardoned (Article 156).

Bringing together or putting into contact for *zinā* or *liwāṭ* shall be punished with 70 lashes for a man, 75 for a woman, and exile for a period determined by the judge (Articles 165-168).

Accusing someone of sodomy without sufficient proof is to be punished with 80 lashes (Articles 169-171).

The executions of 'homosexuals' after the February 1979 revolution were sharply denounced in Western media. Amnesty International concluded that offences such as sodomy were not always proved according to *šarīʿa* rules.[19]

Many people executed for sodomy were, at the same time, accused of other crimes.[20] According to Irānian officials, the executed were "hardened criminals, who traffic in drugs and who abduct young children and forcibly subject them to the sexual abuse and satisfy their sensual lust, which mostly lead to the murder of their innocent victims."[21] But Amnesty International knows about cases of men prosecuted for sodomy only. Sodomy was no doubt used as a label to denounce persons who were considered criminals, or who were seen as enemies of the Islāmic revolution. Prior to the revolution, Tehran was one of very few cities in the Middle East with a gay subculture, a middle class phenomenon totally incomprehensible to most Ḥumaini supporters.

ʿIrāq

Article 232 of The Baġdad Penal Code of 1918 made rape upon women and sodomy on men and women without consent punishable with penal servitude for a term not exceeding 15 years.

Article 235 made sodomy on a child under the age of 15 punishable with penal servitude or imprisonment for a term not exceeding seven years.

In the Penal Code of 1969[22] Article 232 became Article 394, but Article 235 was redesigned and numbered Article 395. The age of consent was lowered to 14 years and the punishment was raised to a maximum of 10 years imprisonment. If the minor is between 15 and 18 years old and does not resist the act, the adult may be punished with imprisonment of up to seven years. Article 393 imposes a maximum penalty of 15 years imprisonment for sodomy.

Decree nº 488 of the Revolutionary Council (April 24, 1978), punishes sodomy on a blood relative up to the third degree with imprisonment for life.

Jordan (The Hashemite Kingdom of)

The Penal Code of the British Mandate of Palestine (and Transjordan) punished sodomy with a prison term of up to 10 years—

and with a sentence of up to 14 years for sodomy with a male person under the age of 16.[23]

The Penal Code of 1951[24] makes no distinction between sexual intercourse by persons of the same sex or persons of different sexes. Article 298 punishes sexual intercourse with persons under the age of 16 (male or female) by forced labor for three to 15 years, while the punishment for sex with male or female under the age of 13 must not be less than five years imprisonment.

The Jordanian Penal Code is officially still applied in the West Bank, which was occupied by Israel in 1967, but not in (East) Jerusalem, which was annexed.

Kuwait

In 1956, the British authorities enacted a Penal Code to replace the Indian Penal Code; sodomy was punishable with imprisonment not exceeding 10 years, with or without corporal punishment.[25]

In 1960 a new Code written by ʿAbdarrazzāq as-Sanhūrī was adopted. This Egyptian jurist aimed at legislation both conforming to the underlying principles of Islamic law and to the Natural Laws as developed in the West.[26] This code was amended by Law nº 76 of 1976.

Article 192 of 1960 punished sexual intercourse with a boy or a girl under the age of 18 (without force or tricks) with imprisonment of up to five years and a fine up to 5,000 Rubiya. If the culprit is directly related, is the guardian or the employer of the victim the punishment may not exceed seven years and 7,000 Rubiya.

Article 193 punished sexual intercourse between men over the age of 18 with imprisonment of up to three years and a fine up to 3,000 Rubiya.[27]

In 1976 the age of consent was raised to 21 years in both Articles, the option to impose a fine was abolished and the prison term maximum was extended to 10 years for sex with minors (15 years if the victim is dependent), and seven years for sex by consenting men.

Lebanon

Article 519 of the Penal Code of March 1, 1943,[28] decrees prison of up to six months for indecent acts with males or females under the age of 15.

Article 523 of the Penal Code makes habitual sexual intercourse with males or females under 21 punishable with a fine of 25 to 250 pounds.

Article 534 makes sodomy punishable with imprisonment not exceeding one year.[29]

Libya

In 1953, Libya enacted a Penal Code based upon an Egyptian model (thus, via the Italian Code, influenced by the Code Napoléon).

Law 70 (after the 1969 coup) from October 2, 1973, "Regarding the establishment of the *ḥadd* penalty for *zinā* and modifying some of the provisions of the Penal Law," revives selected *šarīʿa* rules regarding fornication.[30] The definition of *zinā* in Article 1 as intercourse between a man and a woman who are not bound to each other by marriage, does not include sodomy upon males, which in the view of most Mālikī jurists, predominant in Libya, falls under *zinā*, albeit with a stricter punishment: stoning not only for a *muḥṣan*, but for a non-*muḥṣan* as well.

The 'old' Article 407 of the Penal Code[31] dealt with rape; in 1973 it was changed by provision VIII/1, and now states: "Whoever has intercourse with a person with his consent will be punished with his partner by imprisonment of not more than five years." In the Arabic version of the addition the penalization of consensual intercourse is sexually neutral. Presumably, this provision will cover sodomy, as Article 410 was deleted; it had penalized sodomy only where the offenders had committed the act publicly or had been apprehended *in flagrante delicto*, and provided for imprisonment from one to four years. The old Article 407 had provided for punishment of imprisonment of up to 10 years for acts committed by force, deceit, or with minors or mental defectives.

Article 408 of the Penal Code was amended by Article VIII/2 which states: "Whoever commits an indecent act with a person with his consent will be punished with his partner with imprisonment." Article 408 now reaches all consensual acts between adults instead of incidents of sexual acts where there was no consent, with minors or with mental defectives.

Western 'modern' legal procedures have to be followed, not the stricter *šarīʿa* rules (Article X).[32]

Mauritania

Article 331 of the Penal Code of the Federation of French West Africa, of which Mauritania was part before independence in 1960, made sexual abuse of a child under the age of 13 punishable by forced labor. Sub-Article 331.3 allowed a maximum imprisonment of three years and a fine of one million francs for sexual acts with a person of the same sex under the age of 21.[33] This Code was enacted in 1947 and retained under Article 60 of the Mauritanian Constitution.[34]

Morocco

Article 489 of the Penal Code of November 26, 1962,[35] makes lewd behavior or acts against nature with a person of the same sex punishable with imprisonment of between six months to three years and a fine of 120 to 1,000 dirhams.

Oman

Article 33 of the Penal Code makes acts of sodomy and *saḥq* ('lesbianism') punishable with imprisonment from six months to three years. But only acts arousing scandal lead to public prosecution.[36]

Qaṭar

The Indian Penal Code was replaced in 1956 by a new Penal Code.[37] Article 171 prescribes imprisonment not exceeding 10 years, with or without corporal punishment for sodomy.

The 1971 Penal Code[38] differentiates between sodomy between consenting adults (irrespective of sex) and sodomy without consent or with minors. Article 201 punishes the former with up to five years imprisonment, Article 200 imposes a prison term of up to 10 years on a sodomist who raped someone or buggered someone under the age of 16. Whoever sodomises a dependent under 16 can be imprisoned for up to 14 years.

Saʿūdī-ʿArabia

Saʿūdī-ʿArabia is the Muslim country where the *šarīʿa* was always enforced. The Kingdom of Saʿūdī-Arabia is officially committed to the Wahhabi interpretation of Ḥanbalī law. But where expedient, rulings of other sunnī jurisconsuls may be applied.

In 1928, the Judicial Board advised the Muslim judges to look for guidance in two books by the Hanbalite jurist Marʿī ibn Yūsuf al-Karmī al-Maqdisī (d. 1033/1624). In the *ad-Dalīl aṭ-Ṭālib li-Nail al-Muṭālib*,[39] *liwāṭ* is to be treated like fornication, and must be punished in the same way. If *muḥṣan* and free, one must be stoned to death, while a free bachelor must be whipped 100 lashes and banished for a year. Ibn Dūyān (1858-1934) a Saʿūdī subject, advises in his 'commentary' on the *Dalīl* to put to death both the *muḥṣan* and the non-*muḥṣan*—as proscribed in a well known *hadīt*. A non-Muslim who buggers a Muslim must always be stoned to death.

Sodomy is proved either by the culprit confessing four times or by the testimony of four trustworthy Muslim men. If there are less than four witnesses or one of them is not trustworthy, they are all to be punished with 80 lashes (a slave 40) for slander (*qaḏf*).

Executions for criminal offences in Saʿūdī-Arabia are rarely published, but one execution was widely reported in 1977. On February 25, two men were publicly beheaded (not stoned as the *šarīʿa* requires) for indecently assaulting a boy they had kidnapped.[40] In another incident, a Saʿūdī-ʿArabian who raped and murdered another man was beheaded by sword in a Jeddah public square on October 1, 1981.[41]

Somalia (Democratic Republic)

The Indian Penal Code was applied in British Somalia from 1925 to 1973, when a Somali Penal Code was adopted.[42] Article 409[43] punishes sexual intercourse with a person of the same sex with imprisonment from three months to three years, and an act of lust different from sexual intercourse with prison from two months to two years.

Article 400 stipulates imprisonment of 80 months to 20 years for sodomy committed with violence and of 16 to 80 months for other acts of lust forced on a person of the same sex.

According to Article 410, a security measure may be added to a sentence for homosexual acts. This is normally police surveillance—to guarantee that the person convicted does not engage in these activities again.

The Sudān

In 1899, the Indian Penal Code was introduced.[44] It was replaced by a new Penal Code in 1925, which made normal (Section 317) and 'unnatural' (Section 318) coition with any person or with a dependent of either sex under the age of 16 punishable with imprisonment of up to 14 years.

In 1983 a new penal code was promulgated; ostensibly it is based on the *šarīʿa* without adherence to any special school. Article 316 defines *zinâ* as penetration with the penis (or part thereof) into the vagina or the anus of a person on whom one has no legal right to or as granting permission to someone without legal right to penetrate one's vagina or anus. For a *muḥṣan* capital punishment is prescribed, for a *gair muḥṣan* 100 lashes.[45]

The laws were seldom applied. No cases of executions for sodomy were reported prior to April 1985, when the government of an-Numairi was overthrown and these rules were temporarily put aside. Between September 1983 and April 1985 hundreds of men and women were lashed for 'intended' unlawful heterosexual intercourse, but none, as far as is known, for sodomy. In February the military government of Ḥassan al-Bašīr reinstated *šarīʿa* law.

Syria

Article 505 of the Penal Code of 1949[46] makes indecent acts with either a male or a female under the age of 16 punishable with prison of up to six months. Article 520 sanctions (consensual) sodomy with males, females, or animals with imprisonment of up to a year.

Tunisia

Article 227 of the Penal Code of 1913 (largely modified in 1964[47]) makes indecent acts against minor children punishable with imprisonment of up to five years. According to Article 228 coition with either male or female without consent shall be punished with prison and penal servitude of up to five years—up to 10 years if committed against a minor child, irrespective of consent. Article 230 decrees imprisonment of up to three years for sodomy between consenting adults.

Turkey

The Turkish Penal Code of 1926 is heavily influenced by the Italian Code. There is no special anti-sodomy provision.

Article 414: "Whoever ravishes an infant who has not completed 15 years shall be punished by heavy imprisonment for not less than five years. Where the offense is committed through the use of force, violence or threats, or against an infant who, because of mental or physical defect or on account of a cause other than the perpetrator's action or a fraudulent means used by the perpetrator, was not in a state to resist the offender, the period of heavy imprisonment shall not be less than 10 years."

Article 415: "Whoever commits an action which constitutes a carnal abuse of a minor who has not completed 15 years of age, the offender shall be sentenced to heavy imprisonment for two to four years."

Article 421: "Whoever converses with a woman or a young man in a lewd manner, shall be imprisoned for three months to one year, and whoever molests women or young men in other ways, shall be imprisoned for six months to two years."[48]

The United Arab Emirates

The Indian Penal Code for the Trucial States was replaced by a new one on September 24, 1956.[49]

Article 171 made sodomy punishable with imprisonment not exceeding 10 years, with or without corporal punishment.

Today there is a federal criminal statute, as well as Penal Codes in four of the seven emirates: Dubai,[50] Abū Ẓabī,[51] Ras al-Ḫaima, and Šarǧa.

The Federal Penal Code (FPC, Law nº 3 of 1987) came into force on March 21, 1988. It does not abolish the penal legislation of the emirates, but only repeals "all provisions contrary" to it. Moreover the FPC leaves intact the *šarīʿa* provisions on crimes. The public prosecutor's office will continue to have the discretion to charge a defendant with either a *šarīʿa* crime before a *šarīʿa* court, or a statutory crime under the FPC before a Federal court or under an Emirate statute before a local court.[52]

Article 354 of the FPC is ambiguously phrased:

يعاقب بِالَا عدام

كُل شَخص استِخدم الاكراه في مَواقعة أُنثى او اللِواط مَع ذَكر

In a semi-official translation in use by lawyers in the Emirates this is rendered as: capital punishment for "any individual who forcibly compels a female to carnal copulation or a man to sodomy." However the article can be translated as "Whoever commits rape on a female or sodomy with a male" shall be punished by death.[53]

Article 80 of the Abu Ẓabī Penal Code makes sodomy punishable with imprisonment of up to 14 years. Article 177 of the Penal Code of Dubai imposes imprisonment of up to 10 years on consensual sodomy; article 176 allows a prison term of up to 14 years for sodomy without consent or with a boy under 16.

Most Emīrīs are Sunnis of the Malikī school (except for a Šafiʿītes enclave in Fuğaiara[54]), in which sodomy is regarded as *zinā*, albeit meriting a stricter punishment: both *muḥṣan* and non- *muḥṣan* are to be put to death by stoning.

Yemen

On May 5, 1990 the unification of Yemen was proclaimed. When this book went to the press, no constitution and no unified legal system was in place.

North Yemen (Arab Republic of Yemen)

Although the population of North Yemen is almost equally divided between the Šafiʿī and the Zaidī (law) schools, its legal system is said to be primarily based upon Šafiʿī interpretation of Muslim law.[55] But, there is still no general application of State law.

On sodomy, aš-Šafʿī had two opinions: 1) death by stoning for both partners, or 2) death by stoning for a *muḥṣan* and 100 lashes plus deportation for one year for the non-*muḥṣan*.

Most post-classical jurists, such as Abū Šūğā (d. 499/1106)[56] and Ibn Qāsim al-Ġazzī (d. 918/1528),[57] follow the second opinion. The founder of the (šiʿite) Zaidī branch, Zaid ibn ʿAlī ibn al-Ḥusain (d. 122/740) is said to have said: "If both are *muḥṣan*, they must be put to death by stoning, if both are not, they are to be flogged."[58]

South Yemen (People's Democratic Republic of Yemen)

Most citizens follow the Shafi'i rite. During the Protectorate, the British ruled the greater part of South Yemen indirectly, and the local Šaiḫs applied customary law and/or the *šarīʿa*. The Indian Penal Code was introduced in 1937 only in the Crown Colony of Aden. This was changed in 1955, when the Penal Code for the Persian Gulf was introduced.[59] It made sodomy punishable with imprisonment not exceeding 10 years, with or without corporal punishment.

The Penal Code of the People's Democratic Republic of Yemen of 1976, although influenced by Soviet legislation, does not mention sexual acts between adult males. Article 167 punishes sexual intercourse with a person under 16—male or female—with prison of not less than three years.

NOTES

1. The Syrian constitution stipulates 'only' that the state-president must be a Muslim.

2. In some states, this is not part of the constitution but is written into the introduction of some laws.

3. Sura VII,80; XXVI 165-166; XXIX 27-28.

4. Manohar, V.R.E. and W.W. Chitaley, *The A.I.R. Manual: Unrepealed Central Acts*, Nagpur: All India Reporter 4 1984, p.597.

5. *The Persian Gulf Gazette*, Suppl. 9, London: Her Majesty's Stationary Office, (July 1) 1955, p.86, 89.

6. Age of Consent Laws have History of Errors in *NAMBLA-Bulletin*, IX, 1 (January-February 1988), p.6.

7. Sebastian Beck, *Das Afghanische Strafgesetzbuch vom Jahre 1924*, Berlin: de Gruyter, 1928, p.121.

8. Without place [Lahna], 1310/1892, p.78.

9. Ibrāhīm al-Ḥalabī, Īstanbul, 1836, p.99.

10. Baber Johansen, Eigentum, Familie und Obrigkeit im Hanafitischen Starfrecht in *Welt des Islāms* XIX (1979), p.58.

11. *Journal officiel de la République Algérienne* nº 49 (June 11, 1966).

12. According to this law women must be given away in a marriage and cannot marry on their own and must obtain the authorisation of a husband or a father in order to go to work; polygamy is recognized.

13. *The Persian Gulf Gazette*, Supplement nº 15, London: Her Majesty's Stationary Office, January 29, 1957, p.4.

14. Husain M. Albaharna, *The Arabian Gulf States*, Beirut: Librairie du Liban, [2] 1975, p. xxxviii.

15. Prof. Dr. jur. Dietrich Oehler, *Internationales Strafrecht*, Köln: Carl Heymanns Verlag, p.233n.

16. *Code Pénal et Procedure Pénale*, Cairo: Nasr Misr Press, 1957.

17. Dara Ilzad, *Khomeini's strafwetgeving, wreed of rechvaardig?*, Amsterdam: Private Publication, pp.72-77.

18. Articles 157-164 deal with 'Lesbianism': punishment of a woman of sound mind and free will is hundred lashes. If the act is repeated three times and punishment is enforced, death sentence will be issued the fourth time. Who repents after her own confession or before the valid testimony of the witnesses is given may be pardoned. Two women not related by blood are naked under one cover without good reason, both will be punished to less than hundred lashes. In case of repetition, hundred lashes will be hit the third time.

19. *Law and Human Rights in the Islamic Republic of Iran*, London: Amnesty International Publications, 1980, p.88; AI has no information on whether the death penalty has been applied as a *hadd* punishment or whether as an exercise of discretion in cases where the requirements of proof were not fulfilled.

20. Amnesty listed known cases of death penalty and flogging. In the period February 16, 1979 to August 11, 1979, there were capital punishment for 'sodomy' (3 cases), for 'homosexual rape' (3 cases), for 'homosexual rape' in combination with 'indecent assaults' (6 cases), for 'homosexual rape' combined with 'deluding and misleading children' (1 case), for 'sodomy' combined with 'procuring' and 'adultery' (1 case), and for 'sodomy' combined with 'drug offences' (1 case). One 'victim of homosexual rape' was punished with 100 lashes. One who made two attempts to commit sodomy was punished with 20 lashes. Five foreigners were punished for sodomy with hundred lashes and imprisonment.

21. Cit. by Anonymous, *The Old Hardened Criminal Trick*, in *Campaign*, nº 57.

22. Law nº 111 in *Al-waqā'i' al-'irāqiya* nº 1778 (September 5, 1969).

23. This article existed in Israel until March 24, 1988.

24. *Qanūn al-'uqubāt* (Law nº 85 of 1951), substantially amended by law nº 16/1960, *al-ğarīda ar-rasmīya* nº 14 (May 1, 1960).

25. *The Persian Gulf Gazette*, Supplement nº 14 (October 14, 1956), London: Her Majesty's Stationary Office, p.6.

26. Sanhurī, *Masadir al-haqq fil'l al-islāmī. Dirasa muaqrana bi'l fiqh al-ğarbī*, al-Qāhira: Mu'assarat Aḥmad Raġāb, 1967.

27. Hasan Sadiq al-Masrawī, *Šarḥ, qanūn al-ğaza al-Kuwaitī; al-qism al-hass*, Beirut: al-Maktab as-sarai, 1970, pp.215-216.

28. *Journal Officiel de la République Libanaise* 1943 nº 4075; or see *Les Codes Libanais en Textes Français* (collection Elie J. Boustany, with introduction by M. Fouad Ammoun), Beirut: Librairies Antoine, 1956, pp.284-285.

29. Under the laws governing prostitution, sexual acts between males in brothels are forbidden and, in addition to the penalties for prostitution, the brothel may be closed for one week to six months. Prostitution is legal for registered women. Male prostitutes may be sentenced to imprisonment from two to six months.

30. Ann Elizabeth Mayer, *Libyan Legislation in Defense of Arabo-Islamic Sexual Mores*, in *The American Journal of Comparative Law*, vol. 28, nº2, spring 1980, pp.287-313.

31. *Gazette Officiale del Regno . . . di Libia*, Codice Penale 28.2.1954, p. 117.

32. Cf. the *Second ILGA Pink Book*, Utrecht, 1988: "Section 114 of the Military Penal Code punishes each soldier, who attempts or performs homosexual acts, with up to 5 years imprisonment."

33. Bouvenet, Gaston-Jean and Paul Hutin, *Recueil annoté des Textes de Droit Pénal . . . Applicable en Afrique occidentale Française*, Paris: Edition de l'Union Française, 1955.

34. Michael Joel, Mauritania, in *International Encyclopedia of Comparative Law*, Vol. 1 (ed. Viktor Knapp), The Hague: Mouton; Tübingen: J.c.B. Mohr, 1972, p.55.

35. *Al-ğarida ar-rasmiya li'l mamlakat al-maġribiya* (June 5, 1963).

36. *IGA Pink Book 1985*, Amsterdam; Acts of lesbianism among ancestors or descendants or among sisters, shall not be pursued upon a complaint by a relative or a brother-in-law thereof, up to grade four.

37. *The Persian Gulf Gazette*, Supplement nº 14 (October 15, 1956), London: Her Majesty's Stationary Office, p.8.

38. *Qanūn al-ʿuqubāt* (Law nº 14 of August 25, 1971), in *al-ğarīda ar-rasmīya 7/1971* (August 3, 1971), Doha.

39. George M. Baroody, *Crime and Punishment under Islamic Law*, Oxford: Regency Press, 1961, [2] 1979, pp.56-68.

40. *Amnesty International Report 1977*, London: Amnesty International Publications, p.312.

41. *Saudi beheaded*, in *The Gurdian*, London, October 3, 1981.

42. J.N.D. Anderson, *Islamic Law in Africa*, London, 1954. p.40 (Colonial Research Publications nº 16).

43. Martin R. Ganzglass, *The Penal Code of the Somali Democratic Republic*, New Brunswick (N.J.): Rutgers University Press, pp.444-447.

44. Prof Dr. jur. Dietrich Oehler, *Internationales Strafrecht*, Köln: Carl Heymanns Verlag, p.223n.

45. *Qanūn al- ʿuqubāt*, Khartum: Military Printing Press, 1983. Articles 216, 218.

46. *Recueil des Lois Syriennes et de la Législation Financière*, Supplement nº 4, Code Pénal (decret législatif nº 148 du 22.6.1949) Damascus 1956, pp. 101-103.

47. A. Guiraud, *Code Pénal Tunisien Annoté suivi des Textes de Répression en Tunisie*, Librairie du Recueil Sirey, Paris, p.80.

48. *The Turkish Criminal Code*, translation: Orhan Sepiçi and Muṣtafa Ovaçik, ed.: Nevzat Gürelli, South Hackensack: Fred B. Rothman, 1965.

49. *The Persian Gulf Gazette*, Supplement nº 14 (October 15, 1956), London: Her Majesty's Stationary Office, 1956, p.12.

50. *al-ğarīda ar-rasmīya* nº 2/1970.

51. *al-ğarīda ar-rasmīya* nº 77/1970 (1.10.1977).

52. Charles S. Laubach, *United Arab Emirates: the New Federal Penal Code* in *Middle East Executive Reports*, XI,3 (March 1988), Washington D.C. pp. 9,21-23.

53. To those who do not read Arabic I give a word by word translation of

the two readings of this sentence: shall be punished by death every person who commits coercion in intercourse [with a] female or who commits sodomy with a male *or* shall be punished by death every person who commits coercion in intercourse [with a] female [or who commits coercion in] sodomy with a male.

54. Richard F. Nyrop et al., *Area Hand Book for the Persian Gulf States*, Washington D.C.: U.S. Government Printing Office, 1977, p.54.

55. Richard F. Nyrop et al., *Area Handbook of the Yemens*, Washington D.C.: U.S. Government Printing Office, 1977, p.220.

56. Ed./trad. L.W.C. van den Berg, Leiden: Brill, 1894, pp.574-577.

57. Ibn Qāsim al-Gazzi: *Fatḥ al-Qarīb*, ed./trad. L.W.C. van den Berg, Batavia: Imprimerie du Gouvernement, vol. III, 1884, p.211.

58. *Muǧmuʿ al-fiqh*, ed. Eugenio Griffini, Milano: Ulrich Hoepli, 1919.

59. Dilger, Konrad, *Die Rolle des Islamischen Rechts im Ostafrikanischen Raum* in *Jahrbuch für Afrikanisches Recht* Vol.2F, Heidelberg: C.F. Müller, 1981.

Liwāṭ

Charles Pellat

LIWĀṬ (A[rabic]) sodomy. There does exist in Arabic a verb lāta, meaning "to attach oneself, to join oneself to," but liwāṭ appears to be rather a *maṣdar* of *lāṭa* or *lāwaṭa*, denominative of Lūṭ, i.e., Lot. In modern Arabic there are also the terms *liwāṭa*, *mulāwaṭa*, *talawwuṭ*, etc., as well as a large number of euphemisms and of dialectical and slang terms. The homosexual[1] is called lūṭī or *lā'iṭ* (pl. *lāṭa*), or *mulāwiṭ*, when he is the active partner, although the distinction is often difficult to establish[2]; the receptive is *ma'būn*, and his perversion, *ubna*. Among the synonyms, the most common is *mukhannath*, generally translated as "effeminate," although in normal usage it refers to the genuine hermaphrodite[3] (see A. Bouhdiba, *La sexualité en Islam*, Paris 1975, 55-7). In the Muslim West in the Middle Ages, a special term, *ḥāwī* (pl. *ḥiwā*) was used in reference to professional male prostitutes.

In a number of verses of the *Ḳur'ān* relating to Lot and his people,[4] the word *fāḥisha*, which may be rendered as "depravity," is clearly an allusion to the vice in question,[5] but this is even more strongly indicated by the pejorative nature of the remarks and questions,[a] attributed to this prophet: *inna-kum lata'tūna l-ridjāla shahwat^{an} min dūni'l-nisā', bal antum ḳawm^{un} musrifūn*; "You commit the carnal act, in lust, with men and not with women, you are indeed an impious people" (VII, 79/81) *a-inna-kum lata'-tūna'l-ridjāla*? (XXVII, 55/54) and *a-ta'-tūna'l-dhukrāna*? (XXVI, 165). The punishment inflicted upon the people of Lot, in the

---

Charles Pellat is one of the editors of *The Encyclopedia of Islam*, in which this article was anonymously published. It has been annotated by Arno Schmitt.

[a]This reads in the original French: «indique par une invective et des interrogations mises dans la bouche de ce prophète» (indicated by a curse and questions concerning their moral conduct attributed to the prophet).

Kur'ān as in the Bible (Gen., XIX, 1-23) leaves no doubt as to the way in which sodomy should be regarded by Islam, even though it is not explicitly condemned by the Holy Book, which indeed allows a certain ambiguity in passages where the believers are promised that in paradise they will be attended by menservants (*ghilmān*, LII, 24; *wildān*, LVI, 17, LXXVI, 19).

The statements of *ḥadīth* are, on the other hand, perfectly clear and particularly harsh, as is noted by an-Nuwayrī who, in his *Nihāya* (ii, 204-10), has conveniently collected them together[6] with the addition of the opinions of the Companions and the *fuḳahā'* on the subject. The Prophet is alleged to have said that what he feared most for his community were the practises of the people of Lot (although he seems to have expressed the same idea in regard to wine and to female seduction *Nihāya*, ii, 198). According to him, both the active and the passive agent[b] must be killed (*yuḳtal/uḳtulū' l-fā'il wa'l-maf'ūl bihi*, terms which were subsequently to be applied, in grammar, to the subject and the direct object[7]) or, more precisely, subjected to the punishment prescribed for the man guilty of *zinā'*,[8] the fornicator, that is, death by stoning (*fa-rdjumū'l-a'lā wa'l-asfal*).[9] The man who sodomises another or inflicts the same treatment on a woman,[10] will on the Day of Resurrection be regarded as more reprehensible than carrion; needless to say, he will suffer eternal damnation, unless he obtains pardon through repentance. The lustful kissing[c] of an adolescent is enough to earn a thousand years in Hell.

By the very fact of their existence, these *ḥadīths* show that, while probably not very common in Bedouin society, homosexuality was not totally unknown in Arabia of the pre-Islamic period.[11] For proof of this, one need look no further than the story of Dhū Nūwās, who was compelled to kill Dhū Shanātir in order to escape his advances. Proverbs of the form *alwaṭ min* . . . (al-Maydānī, ii, 205) testify to the antiquity of the term and of the idea which it expresses; al-Maydānī cites the expression *alwaṭ min Dubb*, making the last word ("bear") into a proper name; similarly al-Djāḥiẓ,

---

[b]passive agent = patiens agens (+ = −).

[c]Here the English translation improves on the original: «Un *simple* baiser donné *avec concupiscence*»; a kiss is either simple or lustful.

(*Mufākharat al-djawārī wal '-ġilmān* in *Rasā'il al-Djāḥiẓ*, ed. Hārūn, ii, 136-7) quotes a Ḥidjāzī proverb, *alwaṭ min Dīk* ("cock") would also be the name of a person; these coincidences are curious, to say the least.[12] Whatever the case may be, animals are not exempt from this vice: al-Djāḥiẓ himself[13] (*Ḥayawān*, ii, 204) cites the example of a *ma'būn* horse, perhaps castrated at an early age, which pursued male horses, mules, and donkeys. The same author seems to have been the first to speak (ibid., vii, 178) of a fabulous animal, the *ʿudār*,[14] which was in the habit of assaulting the men whom it encountered; its victims suffered a worm-infected anus and died as a result (cf. al-Masʿūdī, *Murudj*, iii, 319-20 = § 1203). In his *Mufākhara*, he also mentions a mawlā of Khuzāʿa, Maymūn b. Zaid b. Tharwān, who was a *lā'iṭ* in Kūfa, and who became proverbial under the nickname of Siyāh, but was apparently viewed with indulgence that spared him punishment.

However, in the course of the first/seventh century, a number of precise cases of *lāṭa* subjected to exemplary penalties are reported, especially by[15] al-Djāḥiẓ and an-Nuwayrī. Abū Bakr condemned a homosexual to be buried beneath the débris of a wall,[16] and prescribed burning alive as the penalty for all those guilty of such practises; in this respect he was followed by ʿAbd Allāh b. al-Zubayr and Hishām b. ʿAbd al-Malik. For his part, ʿAlī b. Abī Ṭālib ordered the stoning of a *lūṭī* and had another thrown headfirst from the top of a minaret[17]; according to Ibn ʿAbbās, this last punishment must be followed by stoning. ʿAbd Allāh b. ʿUmar went a step beyond the condemnation predicted by the Prophet, reckoning that these people would be resurrected in the form of monkeys and pigs. The famous letter from an Umayyad caliph [see Khaṣī, IV, 1087b] ordering the governor of Mecca or of Medina to "hold a census" of the *mukhannathūn* of the town corresponds to a real situation, even if the tradition itself is contrived.[18]

In fact, the increase in prosperity brought about by the rich flow of spoils from the conquered land was accompanied, paradoxically, by the corruption of morals in the two holy cities. As regards the subject which concerns us here, information relating to the development of music and song reveals the presence of *mukhannathūn*, who were apparently for the most part of foreign origin. It may thus be assumed that from this time homosexuality became less of a rarity as the result of a rapid process of acculturation. A defender of paedophiles, of lovers of *ghilmān*, depicted in the *Mufākhara* (ii, 116) of al-Djāḥiẓ, observes in effect that natural love is a feature of Bedouin culture and of simple morality and that if the ancient Arab glorified woman, this was because they knew nothing of the redefined pleasures of this world, which are only to be encountered in a highly civilised society.

All the same, it is not impossible that the decisive impulse came with the arrival of the ʿAbbāsīd army from Khurāsān (cf. A. Mez, *Renaissance*, Eng. tr., 358)[19] and that homosexuality subsequently spread more widely under the new dynasty. In fact, tradition attributes to al-Amīn tastes so depraved [sic] that his mother, Umm Djaʿfar, was obliged [sic] to procure for him slave women with the physical characteristics sought after by *lāṭa* among boys and to dress them in masculine clothing,[d] in the hope of inducing him to accept more conventional morals[e] (al-Masʿūdī, *Murūdj*, viii, 299-300 = §§ 3451-2). It was no doubt such episodes that gave rise to the fashion for "masculine girls," *ghulāmiyyāt*, a trend widely reflected in literature (see Ḥ. Zayyāt, *al-Marʾa al-ghulāmiyya fi 'l-Islām*, in *Machriq* 1956). In Ifrīḳa, the Aghlabīd Ibrāhīm II was surrounded by some sixty catamites, whom he treated in a most horrific manner[f] (see M. Talbi, *Émirat aghlabide*, 306, 317).[20] At Cordoba, ʿAbd al-Raḥmān III had executed a young lad from Léon who was held as a hostage, the future St. Pelagius (Pelayo), because he had refused his advances (Simonet, *Historia de los Mozárabes*, 542; see also Ch.E. Dufourcq, *La vie quotidienne dans l'Europe médiévale sous la domination arabe*, Paris, 1987, 117-18). Homosexual tendencies are attributed to al-Muʿtaṣim and to some of his successors, and it is probable that this is not a case of slander designed to justify a vice vigorously opposed by the *fuḳahāʾ*.[21]

In general the *ḥadīth* relating to the punishment of the *lūṭī* provides the base for the opinions of jurists, but a distinction tends to

---

[d]should be: boys' clothes.

[e]French: pour l'engager à revenir à des moeurs plus normal.

[f]In the original «à qui il fit . . . subir un sort horrible», i.e., a painful death.

be made, in the application of the legal sanction (*ḥadd*), according to whether the culprit is muḥṣan or not, that is in practice[g] whether he is married or celibate. Ibn Ḥanbal and his followers appear [sic] to be the most severe, since they insist that in all cases the culprit must be put to death by stoning,[22] while the other schools are in general content with flagellation, with or without banishment, if the man is not *muḥṣan*; it should be noted in addition that it is sometimes[23] recommended that the prescribed penalty (100 strokes) should not be applied in full, and Ibn Ḥazm goes so far as to reduce the number of strokes to 10.[24] These variations correspond to the uncertainties surrounding the definition of the penalty[25] to be imposed for fornication, but also betray a tendency toward indulgence; moreover, since proof is always difficult to establish, there is little likelihood of the punishment actually being applied. These circumstances do not prevent moral pundits from considering illegal a lustful glance in the direction of a beardless youth (*amrad*), and the Ḥanbalīs forbid men to walk in the street with women or with adolescents (Mez, *Renaissance*, Eng. tr., 362).[26]

The legal provisions set out above are thus to a large extent theoretical, since homosexual relations have always been tolerated. They were common in religious brotherhoods and in educational institutions (see A. Bouhdiba, *op. laud.*, 146), and schoolmasters had an unenviable reputation in this respect, as is shown by many anecdotes. The nudity of the public baths did nothing to discourage such practises, and the paragraph devoted by H. Pérès (*Poésie andalouse*, 341-3) to homosexuality in al-Andalus refers specially to the *ḥammām*.[h]

As regard woman . . .[27]

Besides female prostitution (bighā'), there is abundant evidence of male prostitution. It is not known how much credence should be attached to an allegation by Ibn Ḥawḳal[28] (93, 95, tr. Kramers-Wiet, 91, 93), reiterated in part by al-Idrīs (*Nuzha*, ed. Pérès, Algiers 1957, 70; ed. Naples-Rome, iii, 269-70), according to

---

[g]Correct translation would be "roughly," "approximately," not "in practice."

[h]In the original: «La nudité des bains publics ne manquait pas non plus de les favoriser, et c'est précisément à propos du *ḥammām* que H. Pérès est ammené à consacrer un paragraphe à l'homosexualité dans al-andalus.»

which the Kutāma Berbers "offer themselves to their guests as a token of hospitality, without any sense of shame," while at Sétif, they are content to offer their male children. Inconsistencies in these passages[29] are such as to cast doubt on the author's claims.

In any case, the presence of professional deviants (*mu'ādjirūn*) in the larger towns has been frequently attested by travellers (see G.H. Bousquet, *L'éthique sexuelle de l'Islam*, Paris 1953, 59).[30] Mention has been made of transvestites, for example in Bougie (Idrīs, *Zīrides*, 329, 591[31]), in Tunis (R. Brunschvig, *Ḥafṣides*, ii, 173[32]) where Leo Africanus (tr. Épaulard, 385[33]) saw young boys prostituting themselves, in Fez, where the same author encounters what he calls cheua (= *ḥiwā*, a term of particularly common usage in Spain; see Dozy, *Suppl.*) living with men in hostelries. Such statements cover such a broad expanse of time that they cannot but be a reflection of a permanent situation which has, moreover, persisted into the present day (see, e.g., Bouhdiba, *op. laud.*, 233). It need hardly be said that the authors of works of ḥisba[34] utterly deplore these deviants and the moral corruptions for which they are responsible, but not one of them is so severe as to demand for them the capital penalty ordained by the aforementioned *ḥadīth*. According to Ibn ʿAbidūn (Lévi-Provençal, *Séville musulmane*, Paris 1947, § 170), the ḥiwā are to be expelled from the town and severely punished if they return, since they are accursed by Allah and of the whole people; al-Sakkaṭī (*Manuel hispanique de ḥisba*, ed. Colin and Lévi-Provençal, Paris 1931, 68, and gloss., 26; Spanish translation by Chalmeta, in *al-Andalus*, 1968ff., § 161) speaks only of *mukhannathūn* (singers disguised as women[i]), whom he forbids to wear their hair long over the temples or to attend banquets and funerals (see also Lévi-Provençal, *Trois traités hispanique de ḥisba*, Cairo 1953, 123). Although the repression of *liwāṭ*, in the strict sense of the word, forms a part of the general censorship of morals, these works contain few specific references to it.

It should be said that this phenomenon, while provoking the

---

[i]Not "disguised as women," but 'in partly female outfit': the *muhannatūn* were not mistaken for women, but taken as unmanly men. Similarly, the *ġulamiyāt* did not conceal their being girls.

disapproval of a number of moralists loyal to the tradition of the Prophet,[35] has for the most part been viewed with indulgence—if not actively once condoned—even in circles which would appear to be furthest from it.

First, homosexuality was a theme favoured by libertine poets who, especially from the first/seventh century onwards, glorified homosexual love quite shamelessly, often in terms of intolerable [sic] obscenity; in the interminable list of these poets, the first place belongs without doubt to Abū Nūwās who, even without the dedication of the *1001 Nights* (see N. Elisséeff, *Thèmes et motifs*, 150) plays a role of unassailable eminence in this regard. His master Wāliba b. al-Khubāb, who is thought to have debauched him, Khusayn b. al-Dakhkhāk, Muṭī b. Iyās and a great number of others, were imitated and sometimes overtaken by exponents of *mudjūn* and of *sukhf*, which Ibn al-Khadjdjādj made his specialty, as well as by Ibn Ḳuzman in his celebrated *zadjals*.

On the other hand, there are a great many poets who have not hesitated, at some point or other in their career, to sing the praises of a youth, in many cases no doubt, less from personal taste than from the desire to conform artificially with a general trend. In fact care should be taken not to accuse all such writers of libertinism, for it was conventional practice to glorify wine, women, and favourites, without becoming personally involved in debauchery or violating the rules of Islamic ethics. We may cite, as a simple-[minded] example, the theme of *dabīb*, of "crawling,"[36] appropriate perhaps for an Imru' al-Ḳays who lived in a society where it was possible to crawl under the tent in order to approach woman, but purely conventional in the case of a city-dweller like Ibn Shuhayd who, unlike the pre-Islamic poet, uses (*apud* Ibn Bassam, *Dakhira*, i/1, 244), in poetry of a high standard of sophistication, the masculine form to designate the person in question, whose sex thus remains undefined.[37] Leaving aside the mystics, who frequently adopt an unequivocal posture, the use, by poets whose morality is not suspect, of the masculine form in their love poems, derives less from a desire to shock than from a sense of modesty and from respect for a tradition that was reckoned to be harmless, a tradition maintaining an ambiguity universally accepted and appreciated.

In the sphere of prose, the most significant, if not the oldest writing, is certainly the *Mufākharat al-djawārī wa'l-ghilmān* of al-Djāḥiẓ who, always prone to cultivate the genre of munāẓara, debate,[38] of which he is one of the pioneers in Arabic literature, presents in the form of a stylised [sic] dialogue arguments exchanged between homosexuals and men of normal sexuality.[39] So as to leave no doubt as to his own tastes, this author saw fit to publish a *Risāla fī tafḍīl al baṭn ʿalā 'l-ẓahr* (ed. Pellat, in the Ḥawliyyāt of the University of Tunis, xiii, 183-92) in which he plays on the different meanings of *baṭn*—"stomach" and *ẓahr*—"back" in order to demonstrate, with a great deal of humour, the superiority of the former; he goes so far as to attribute to sodomy the destruction of the people of Thamūd, which is thus accorded the same status as the people of Lot.

In the *Mufākhara*, there are a number of anecdotes which testify to the popularity of stories of lāṭa from the third/ninth century; these were to find a place in collections compiled in later times for the entertainments of what were, in appearance at least, the most puritanical sections of society. A characteristic manifestation of this somewhat perverse taste is encountered in the work of al-Tawḥī-dī, who devotes a chapter of *Imtāʿ*, the eighteenth night (ii, 50 to mudjūn) and naturally tells the story of lūṭī (tr. Bouhdiba, *op. laud.*, 158).[40]

The example set by al-Djāḥiẓ in his *Mufākhara* has been followed by quite serious authors who have left analogous writings, among which we may mention *al-Wasāṭa bayn al-zunāt wa'l-lāṭa* by Ibn Hindū (see Brockelmann [*Geschichte der Arabischen Literatur*], S I, 426) and the *Kitāb al-Ḥikāyāt* by Badr al-Dīn al-ʿAynī (see Ṣ. al-Munadjdjidj, in *RIMA*, iii, 335). In addition, the vice in question inspired a specialised literature all its own, notably consisting of advice on techniques of seducing young men (see Ṣ. al-Munadjdjidj, *al-Ḥayāt al-djinsiyya*, 52-4). The writers of works of eroticism mostly devote some space to sodomy; on this point, the most characteristic works are without doubt the *Nuzhat al-albāb fi-mā lā yūğad fī kitāb* (Brockelmann, I, 495, S I, 904) of al-Tīfāshī and the *Našwat al-sakrān* of Muḥammad Ṣādiḳ Ḥasan Khān (Īstanbul 1296/1878; see Bouhdiba, 178).[41]

In the *Mufākhara* of al-Djāḥiẓ, which has nothing in common with the preceding works, the advocate for the *djawārī* claims (ii, 104) that there has never been a case recorded in which love for a youth has proved fatal, while tradition is full of examples of heterosexuals who have pined away, lost their reason, or died for love. However, there are apparently authentic accounts which contradict this assertion.[42] Al-Ḍabbī (*Buġya*, no. 462; tr. Lévi-Provençal, *En relisant "le Collier de la Colombe"* in *al-Andalus*, xv/2, 363-8) relates, after Ibn Ḥazm (although the text of the *Ṭawk al-ḥamāma*, ed. and tr. L. Bercher, is quite perceptibly different): "the incredible adventure . . . of a certain Aḥmad b. Kulayb, poet and grammarian of Cordova who, in 426/1035, died of grief because one of his fellow-citizens, a member of the Andalusian patrician class, persisted in rejecting his advances" (Lévi-Provençal, *Hist.Esp.*, iii, 445); the same story is told by Yāḳūt (*Irshād*, ii, 19 ff. = *Udabā'*, iv, 109 ff.; cf. Mez, *Renaissance*, Eng. tr., 359-60) who also relates (ii, 23 ff. = iv, 115ff.; cf. Mez, 360-1), after al-Ṣanawbarī, the story of a bookseller of Edessa (al-Ruhā) named Saʿd, whose shop was a literary salon frequented by poets and in particular by a young Christian called ʿĪsā. Saʿd developed a violent passion for the latter, and did not cease pursuing him and dedicating poems to him. ʿĪsā became a monk, and, finally denied access to the monastery, Saʿd set fire to all his possessions and became a vagrant. He died eventually of consumption, but the governor of the town accused the monks of having killed him and condemned the young man to death. The punishment was averted following the payment of a large sum of money, but when ʿĪsā went to visit his parents, the local children pelted him with stones and called him an assassin. A third story (Yāḳūt, *Irshād*, ii, 15ff. = *Udabā'*, iv, 122ff.) tells of a poet in love with a young monk who pines away with grief and dies the very moment that he meets the object of his infatuation.

From anecdotes such as these one gains the impression, on the one hand, that the authorities and the people did not regard the inclinations of these homosexuals as immoral, and on the other, that monasteries and monks played an inauspicious role.[43] It is quite clear that poetry and works such as the *Diyāraāt* of al-Shābushtī regard monasteries as places of debauchery frequented by lovers of forbidden delights. One must, however, proceed with caution, because once again we are faced with a poetic theme whose treatment is analogous to that of the glorification of unnatural love by poets who are influenced more by respect for a tradition than by any desire to become personally involved in the acts to which they refer. In this context, the adventure of the Andalusian poet al-Ramādī, the account of which is borrowed by H. Pérès (*Poésie anadalouse*, 278-9) from a work of dubious authenticity, the *maṭmaḥ al-anfus* of Ibn Khāḳān, seem to us no more authentic than the braggings of Ibn Shuhayd, in a poem composed in imitation of Abū Nūwās (H. Pérès, *op. laud.*, 277-8).

The fact remains that in the Middle Ages, many attacks on Islam by Christians were based on the frequency of homosexual relations which, in their view, were permitted by the *Ḳur'ān* and which characterised the behaviour of Muslims; they based this opinion on verse 20/16 of Sūra IV which they misinterpreted[44] as referring to sodomy, without taking account of the condemnation of "depravity" which it contains (see N. Daniel, *Islam and the West, the making of an image*, Edinburgh 1960, 141-5).

It is indeed difficult to measure precisely the extent of the phenomenon, but it should be recognised that the separation of the sexes, which is a particular feature of Islam, has played a significant role in promoting it (cf. Brunschvig, *Ḥafṣides*, ii, 173), among women[45] as much as among men, and the precautions taken against such behaviour (al-Nuwayrī, for example, entitles the chapter cited above *al-taḥdhīr min al-liwāṭ*[j]) did not succeed in preventing it. It is now known that homosexuality, once regarded as a punishable offence, is caused as much by genetic as by social and psychological factors, but it seems that in the event[k] the latter have played the leading role in the proliferation of what remains, to a large extent, a vice.

---

[j] 'Cautioning against buggery.'

[k] Replace "in the event" by 'in this case'; the French original has «en l'occurrence».

NOTES

1. Although the title is *liwāṭ*/sodomy the article deals in fact with three subjects: male homosexuality, female homosexuality, and sodomy with women.

2. If "active" is meant to mean 'more actively pursuing a mate or being more active during the act,' this definition is wrong. If "active" stands here for 'penetrating' and "passive" for 'taking the penis in,' the difference is hardly difficult to perceive—at least in the original texts; pre-modern Arabic does not even have a word obscuring this difference.

3. Not every "penetrated man"—mostly called *malūṭ bihi*/*maʿfūl bihi*—is *maʾbūn*. The *maʾbūn*—like the *ḥalaqī*—likes to get penetrated. The *muḫannaṯ* is effeminate, he displays some female dress and behavior; the word is not synonymous to *maʾbūn* although many *muḫannaṯūn* are/were *maʾbūnīn*. The hermaphrodite is most often called *ḫunṯa*, pl. *ḫināṯ, ḫanāṯa*.

4. *qaum Lūṭ* should not be rendered as "his people" but as "the people to which he was sent."

5. Although the EI should be a work of reference for the next 30 years, the verses in which *fāḥiša* is used in the context of Lūṭ are not given (IV 15,16; VII 80-84, XXIX 28-35); the story of Lūṭ and 'his' people is further mentioned in: XI 77-81; XV 58-77; XXI 78,79; XXXVII 133-136; L 13, LIII 53; LIV 33-40.

6. Conf.: Lois Anita Giffen: *Theory of profane Love among the Arabs*, New York, 1971, pp. 146,147: "In (the) encyclopaedia (*Nihāyat al-arab fi funūn al-adab*) by Abū'l ʿAbbās Aḥmad ibn ʿAbdalwahāb an-Nuwairī (d. 732/1332) the greater part of Chapter Three of Part One of the Second *ann* is devoted to love theory. I have found that all this material, from the beginning of Chapter Three through the section on the temporal and eternal punishments due to sodomy (*al-liwāṭ*), is material copied of the *Damm al-Hawā* of Ibn al-Ǧauzī. Several times he cites Ibn al-Ǧauzī and his book in such a way that one would think that only that immediate passage was taken from Ibn al-Ǧauzī, whereas, in fact, everything else is, too. In most cases, Nuwairī drops the *asanīd* found in the *Damm*, and he sometimes alters the order of the presentation. However, the copied segments are word for word the same, except for some introductory lines at the beginning of a new subject where he may abbreviate slightly the words of introduction provided by Ibn al-Ǧauzī." (transcription altered a.s.) In the Part on *liwāṭ* an-Nuwairī keeps even the order of presentation and parts of the *asanīd* (conf. *Damm al-hawā*, ed. Muṣṭafa ʿAbdalwāhid, al-Qāhira, 1381/1962, pp. 192sq.).

7. Pellat's "subsequently" presupposes that the *aḥādīṯ* are older than Arabic Grammar or . . . see note 11.

8. " . . . the punishment prescribed for the man guilty of *zināʾ*" is the same as the one for women guilty of *zināʾ*.

9. *raǧm* and *ḥadd az-zināʿ* are not equivalent as Pellat's "more precisely" implies: *ḥadd az-zināʿ* signifies for a *bikr* (i.e., somebody who never had lawful intercourse) 100 lashes, not stoning/*raǧm*.

10. Note that here Pellat really treats *liwāṭ* while he normally treats homosexuality.

11. (See note 7) . . . earlier than Muḥammad's delivering of his message of God. While most scholars take the bulk of *ḥadīṯ* to be much younger than Muḥammad's life time, Pellat places them even in the pre-Islāmic part of his life. On the questions of *ḥadīṯ* and transmission of 'knowledge' in early Islām cf.: James A. Bellamy: Sex and Society in Islamic Popular Literature in *Society and the Sexes in Medieval Islam* (ed. A.L. Sayyid-Marsot), Malibu: Udena, 1976. p.37.

Régis Blachère (*Histoire de la littérature arabe*, Paris, 1952-1966; Regards sur la littérature narative in *Semitica* VI, 1956. pp. 76-86); R. Sellheim (*Sprichwörtersammlungen*, 1954; Abū ʿAlī al-Qālī in *Festschrift Bertold Spuler*, Leiden, 1981; Materialien zur arabischen Literaturgeschichte, Wiesbaden, 1976, especially pp.366, 367); S.M. Samuk (*Die historischen Überlieferungen*, Frankfurt, 1978); Fred Leumhuis (*Ms.1075 Tafsīr of the Cairene Dār al-Kutub and Muǧāhid's Tafsīr* in *Proceedings of the 9th Congress of the Union Européene des Arabisants et Islamisants, Amsterdam 1978*, Leiden, 1981. pp.167-180); G. Stauth (*Überlieferung des Korankommentars*, Diss., Giessen, 1969); A. Rippin (*Ibn ʿAbbās* in BSOAS 44, 1981); J. Ruska (*Arabische Alchemisten* I, Heidelberg, 1924); Martin Plessner (*Ǧābir ibn Ḥayyān* in ZDMG 115, 1965).

12. Curious? (in French: *remarcable*). What should we notice?

13. al-Masūdī: *Murūǧ* spells *ġaddār* and does not speak of 'assaulting' but well as being *ḫalaqī*.

14. al-Ǧaḥiẓ further mentions cats, pigs, and donkeys as being *ḫalaqī* (Cheikh Mousa in *Arabica* XXIX, pp.208, 209). Pellat does not tell us whether this 'fact' serves to reveal anal penetration as 'beastlike' or as 'natural.'

15. "Especially by" must be read as 'known to me are'; the reference is to ed. Pellat, p.21; Nihāya, II p.206.

16. It could be that this punishment was chosen because of XI, 82 (*wa amṭaruna ʿalaihā ḥiǧāratan min siǧǧīlin manḍūdin* = and showers down stone of many-layered clay).

17. I never read such a *ḥadīṯ*.

18. The author of this article is Pellat himself. There he wrote: "The famous story is also reported of the letter of Hišām (*Ḥayawān*, i, 121) or of Sulaymān (*al-Aġānī*, ed. Beirut, iv, 275) or of al-Walīd (*ibid*., iv, 278) b. ʿAbd al-Malik ordering the governor of Medina or Mecca to take a census of (*aḥṣi*) the effeminate men of the two holy towns; having read *iḫṣi*, the official had two (or nine of them) castrated, notably the singer al-Dalāl (*al-Aġānī*, iv, 273 ff.) . . . despite the traditions which tend to make it an historical fact, the whole account is, by all appearances, nothing other than a pleasing anecdote, forged to provide evidence of the inconveniences of the Arabic script, but later exploited by anti-Umayyad authors." 2EI, Paris IV p. 1118, Leiden IV p. 1097.

19. For the suggestion, that "true paederasty comes from the east," Mez gives one source: al-Ǧaḥiẓ. Does Pellat wish to pretend a broader data base? Why else secondary sources? Mez, German original p.337; Span. translation: p.427.

20. The sources of aṭ-Ṭālibī's are: an-Nuwairī and aš-Šammāhī.

21. Pellat probably wanted to say that it is not a case of slander, but designed to defend sodomy by attributing it to persons too high placed to attack. Or can anyone make sense of the sentence as it is?

22. Not correct: the Ḥanbali Ibn Qudāmā for example does not prescribe stoning for the *ġair muḥṣin*, whereas Mālik ibn Anas does. The great difference lies not between the Hanbalīs and the rest, but between the Hanafī—not seeing it a case of *ḥadd* at all—and the other schools.

23. It is sometimes . . . by whom?

24. Since Pellat does not name his source, I presume that it is one of the mentioned books: the *Nihāya* of an-Nuwairī; but this author does not write "Ibn Ḥazm", but "*madhab* Ibn Ḥazm" (II 207), i.e., The Spanish Ẓāhirīs. Furthermore it seems important, to point out, that this 'reduction' is no special leniency towards *lūṭīs*; the Ẓāhirīs never allow more than 10 strokes for deeds, for which neither *qur'ān* nor *sunna* fix a punishment.

25. Definition of the 'crime'?

26. German original p.341; Spanish translation p.433.

27. The paragraph does not treat *liwāṭ*—with the exception of the last sentence—but *siḥāq*. It is scandalous that an article entitled "*liwāṭ*," is not treating '*liwāṭ*', but 'homosexuality'!!

28. *Ṣūrat al-arḍ*.

29. Which inconsistencies?

30. There is no such book; 1953 *La morale de l'Islam* was published, 1966 an enlarged edition with the title *L'éthique*. . . . On p.72 Bouhdiba mentions two travellers; one of whose, von Hammer, consecrates one sentence to the subject.

31. Idrīs gives one source (conveniently edited and translated by Lévi-Provençal): *Ahbār al-Mahdī* by Abū Bakr aṣ-Ṣanhāǧī al-Baidaq. I fail to understand why Pellat does not give the Arabic source.

32. Brunschvig's only source for this: Leo Africanus.

33. Leo Africanus = Ḥasan ibn Muḥammad al-Wāssan al-Fāsī (d. around 1600) *The History and Description of Afrika*, translation: Master Pory, ed. Samuel Purchas, London, 1600 as *Pilgrimes in Five Books* vol. III; different edition: London: Henrie Fetherstone, 1625. I p.779.

34. Literary genre of criticism of public morality.

35. Pellat really seems to believe that the *aḥādīṯ* are true sayings of the 'Prophet.'

36. Fucking by trickery and force under cover of darkness and drugs ('against' the victims).

37. There are more things in heaven and earth than are dreamt of in your philosophy. For proof see either the appendix or Ǧaubarīs *K. al-muhtār*, Ibn Falīta's *Rušd*, aṭ-Tīfāšī, who devotes the whole of chapter IX of his *Nuzha* to this subject (in R. Khawam's French translation pp.215-224), many poems by Abū Nuwās or Muḥammad M'rabet: *The Datura Tree*.

38. Cf. E. Wagner, *Die arabische Rangstreitdichtung in der allgemeinen Literaturgeschichte*, Wiesbaden, 1963.

39. Cf. (Pseudo-) Lukian, *Erotes* and from The Arabian Lights: *The Dispute of the Learned Woman and the Lover of boys*.

40. Prof. Pellat has different editions both of Bouhdiba's book and of the *Kitāb al-imtāʿ wa'l muʾānasa* than I have. In my copy an «homme efféminé» resp. a "*muhannat*" is mentioned, the 'opposite' of a *lūṭī*. The person in question cannot be a *lūṭī*, because he is not searching for a beardless youth, but for a hairy one (*Imtā*, ed. Aḥ. Amīn, Bairūt, 1373, 1953, S.52).

41. Why does Pellat write the "most characteristic works," when he means 'the books mentioned by Bouhdiba'? Not only that there are books more characteristic, but the *Našwa* hardly treats pederasty at all.

42. An important word is missing, cf. «d'exemples d'amoureux qui se consument pour leur belle, perdent la raison et meurent . . . dément *après coup* cette assertion.»: contradicts later, disproves afterwards.

43. I deduce from these two anecdotes that convents were hostile to pederasty; ʿIsā thought the monastry to be the only 'safe' place.

44. This Pellat has to prove against Robert Roberts (*Das Familien-, Sklaven- und Erbrecht im Quran*, Leipzig, 1908, S.29; translation: *The Social Laws of the Qoran*, London, 1925), against the Ǧalālain, our contemporaries ʿAlī Yūsuf, and Saiyid Quṭb (and many other Muslim commentators of the *qurʾān*).

45. Buggery among women? That can happen when a European concept is dealt with under an Arab heading/term, when *liwāṭ* just serves as a pretext to deal with homosexuality.

APPENDIX (TO NOTE 36)
DABBĀB / DIB = "CRAWLING"

Be Cautious!

Abū Nūwās: [I observe the boy]
Till sleep's messenger came to him and his eyelids fell
I waited patiently until he dropped limply
Then I crawled to him like a scorpion—at times on my belly
And from the back I entered that what the trousers cover.
Due to my passion for him my spear strayed from its path,
But he felt the nail in his back and sprang up . . .
Finally he lay on me . . .
I fled my head beaten, my ear bleeding . . . . . .
That's what happens to the one who acts on mere assumptions.

German translation in E. Wagner:
Abū Nūwās, Wiesbaden, 1965, p. 106

Be the First!

While in Antiochia an Alexandrian friend and I were invited to a spiritual-mystical concert. The singer was a youth of 15, even more beautiful than the most beautiful Turkish boy slave. Although his father had to be paid 100 Dirhem for an evening, the youth was in high demand. The host for that particular concert had engaged him already several times in order to bugger him—but in vain.

After the concert, when all the guests arranged to sleep, the singer took his place near a wall, next to him the slave and his father—thus making sure that nobody approached him. When everybody slept—or seemed to sleep—my friend crawled to the singer, held a drug in front of his nose and of those near him, put a leather sack between the two boys, and blew it up thus separating them. When there was enough room between them, he let the air go out, folded it neatly and lay down. He tied the singer's garment up, laying part of his body bare, and he started to take care of 'the small opening in front of his eyes' with a lubricant. When he had reached the goal of his desires, he did it again. Then he repeated the operation with the Turk.

When he came back to his sleeping place I complained that he did not share the boys with me. The Alexandrian replied: 'The table is set. Supper is ready.' But I answered: 'I am not used to eating leftovers.' So my friend told me to come to the next concert . . .

Zainaddīn ʿAbdarraḥīm b. ʿUmar ad-Dimašqī al-Ǧaubarī: *Kitāb al-muḥtār fī kašf al-asrār wa-hatk al-astar,* Chapter 26; trad. French by René Khawam: *Le voile arraché,* vol.III, Paris: Phébus, 1980. pp. 167-73

Be Prepared

Somebody who wants to fuck without the consent of the fuckee should not have too big an organ, and also these 13 things:

—a large needle or hook with a long thread (because some boys change their sleeping place when the lights are put out and everybody seems to sleep; with the help of the thread fixed to the garment of the boy the rapist finds his victim)

—a roll of paper (used to blow out candles lit by alarmed men in the room)

—some soft slippers (for both advance and retreat)

—three pebbles (the *dabbīb* throws one against a copper vessel to check whether the boy has fallen into a deep sleep; if not he repeats his action after a while . . .)

—a small bag filled with dust (when the boy sleeps on his back, the *dabbīb* throws some dust into his victim's eyes to make him turn around; when he awakens the rapist can throw dust into his eyes and escape)

—an inflatable leather bag (see the story above)

—a ring and scissors (used to cut a round hole into the boy's garment)

—*sumāq* leaves (chewing them stimulates the production of saliva, necessary to lubricate anus and penis)

—a dildo (to prepare the ass for the penis of flesh)

—a piece of fur attached to a head gear (when the boy grasps to catch the rapist or at least to catch an identifying turban, all he gets is the unknown fur)

—counterfeit coins (to pay the lad if he awakens and protests; in the darkness he cannot distinguish it from good money)

—a small cushion (to be put on the lad's mouth to prevent him from screaming)

—a raw egg (when everything goes wrong the rapist runs back to his place, trousers down, face to the ground and puts some white of the egg between his buttocks: people will pity him for being an earlier victim of the rapist).

Paraphrase of the 9th chapter
of at-Tifašī's *Nuzhat al-albāb*, trad.
René Khawam: *Les délices des coeurs*,
Paris, pp. 215-217

Be On Your Guard!

A modern Moroccan text:

Hamed said he was going to make some coffee. . . . He went into the kitchen. Taking the [Datura] flowers out of his pocket, he dropped them into the pot of water. He stood for a good while watching them as they boiled. He took them out and threw them down the latrine. He used the yellow water in which they had been boiling to make coffee, and he made it very strong. When it was ready, he filled two glasses and took them into the other room. Then he went into the kitchen and got his own coffee and sat down with them.

Mustafa and Abdeslam drank the coffee as they talked. They went on talking, but it was not long before their words began to come out very slowly. And there were long silences between them, until finally Mustafa shut his eyes and rolled over . . . Abdeslam stayed where he was, with his eyes and mouth open . . . Hamed sat down, beside Abdeslam, reached out and unfastened Abdeslam's belt. He began to pull down his trousers. Abdeslam did not move. He got the trousers off, and then he pulled off Abdeslam's shorts as well. Still he did not move. Hamed pushed him and rolled him over onto his belly. He knelt above him and spat between his buttocks. Then he made him pay for the insults . . . When he had finished he went into his room and slept.

Muḥammad M'rabet: *The Datura Tree*
(in *M'hashish*, San Francisco: City Lights Books, 1969)

A Critique of John Boswell's Writings on Muslim Gays

Arno Schmitt

John Boswell's magnum opus, *Christianity, Social Tolerance and Homosexuality*,[1] while loaded with the paraphernalia of scholarship (many footnotes, foreign language quotations, critical remarks on editions and translations of texts, sharp rebuttals of 'hitherto great scholars,' and hints at thousands of problems, which surpass the scope of the book—not his knowledge), is full of inexplicit presuppositions, mistakes, distortions, and tactical omissions. In spite of its philosophical tone, *Towards the long view: Revolutions, Universals and Sexual Categories*[2] is no better.

I undertake to support this opinion on the basis of the passages in these two publications concerning Islam. This restriction is fair, since Boswell started his academic career with two works on Muslims in Spain.[3]

He writes that "most Muslim cultures have treated homosexuality with indifference, if not admiration,"[4] and that Islam generally has a "positive attitude toward gay sexuality"[5] without supplying evidence for these 'facts.'

No sources are given for the following statement: "Almost without exception the classical works of Arabic poetry and prose . . . treat gay people and their sexuality with respect or casual acceptance."[6] Of course, if Boswell has a particular personal canon of classical works in mind, nobody can argue with him, but if we consider 'the (important) works of the classic period of Arabic poetry and prose,' Boswell is wrong (cf. my bibliography not yet published[7]).

For his assertion "much Persian poetry and fiction providing examples of moral love and gay relationships,"[8] Boswell gives no examples.

UNSUBSTANTIATED ASSERTIONS

Possibly the best quotation to show the deficiency of this historian's research is:

> When the Muslims invaded Spain . . . they found many Jews living in Spain, and it is probable that the same was true of gay people, although since no Muslim writer would have considered homosexual preference a matter of note, no mention is made of this.[9]

Totally wrong is his remark: "Note that nearly all the love poetry on pp. 440-80 [of F. Rosenthal's translation of Ibn Ḫaldūn's *Muqaddima*, New York 1958] is written by one man to another." I, at least, could find only one poem from a boon-companion to another and a few poems *about* good-looking boys, but not a single love poem "written by one man to another."

Another case of wishful reading is the sentence in *Christianity* p. 196/7 (in the context of gay love and sexuality): " . . . the kingdom of Valencia has been ruled by a pair of former slaves who had *fallen in love* and risen together the ranks of civil service . . . their love for each other was celebrated in verse by poets . . . " In the footnote Boswell lauds Wilhelm Hoenerbach's German (partial) translation of the Arab history containing this story.[10] But most readers would be astonished at what they can find there: "Behavior and attitude of true friends to an extent surpassing that of twins and lovers . . . constantly together . . . only apart in intercourse with their wives/women (nur im Verkehr mit den Frauen getrennt)."

DISTORTION

Consider this passage in *Christianity* (p. 197) is a clever mixture of distortion and untruth:

> It would be a mistake to imagine this cultural predilection for homosexual eroticism as the result of secularization or religious decline: Spanish Islam was noted for its rigidity in legalistic and

moral matters, produced outstanding jurists and theologians, and was generally ruled by Muslims considered fanatics in the rest of the Islamic world. Homosexual love imagery was a standard currency of Islamic mystical writing both in and out of Spain. Many of the authors of gay erotic poetry on the Iberian peninsula were teachers of the Qur'ān, religious leaders, or judges; almost all [!] wrote conventional religious verse as well as love poetry. Ibn al-Farra', a teacher of the Qur'ān in Almería, addresses amorous verse to his pupils in class and wrote a poem about taking a reluctant lover to court, where the *qāḍī* [i.e. Islamic-law-judge] ruled that the youth must give in to the teacher's advances:

> Then (the judge) indicated to the flowers that they were to be taken.
> And to the mouth that it should be tasted.
> And when my beloved saw him on my side,
> And there was *no longer* any controversy between us,
> He abandoned his resistance, and I enfolded him
> As if I were a *lam* and my lover an *alif* . . . [11]

With regard to this passage I want to remark: First, Spain was not *generally* ruled by 'fanatics.' Second, a casual reader of this paragraph is led to conclude that the religious Muslims of Spain—although generally rigid in matters of law—were lenient with regard to homosexuality. Boswell does not inform the reader that most Spanish Muslim jurists prescribed the death penalty for sodomites, both the 'active' and the 'passive,' both those married (before) and those never married.

A footnote on the previous page is equally misleading: "Male prostitutes *abounded* in Andalusian cities: see 'Le traité d'Ibn Abdun'."[12] Boswell does not explain the character of this treatise; it belongs to a literary genre of lists of blameworthy (i.e., un-Islamic) phenomena to be remedied by the ruler and the community of believers. In the eyes of these critics of morals a single prostitute is one too many. Therefore these books tell more about their authors than about prostitution. But Boswell takes the description uncritically, without noting the existence of these fervent critics of male-male sex.

Third, Boswell gives the impression that a religious court ruled that a youth must give in to his teacher's advances. It is more correct to say that a) this is not a religious (i.e., state) court, but a fictitious one, a court of love (it is Boswell not Ibn al-Farra' who talks of a *qāḍī*), b) the judge does not indicate "to the mouth that it should be tasted," but to the saliva that it should be sucked, c) the youth does not see that there is no longer any controversy between his teacher and the judge; the two men could well have been in agreement all along ('no longer' is added by Boswell), d) Boswell renders the Arabic 'my love' wrongly as 'lover,' thus blurring the opposition between 'lover' and 'loved one.'

Boswell uses technically correct but misleading sentences, for example *Christianity* p. 194: "Although the Qur'ān and early religious writings of Islam display mildly negative attitudes toward homosexuality, Islamic society has generally ignored these deprecations . . . "[13]

It is correct that both Qur'ān and early religious writings display a mildly negative attitude towards male-male sex, but only in comparison with later religious writings. The tone of disapproval becomes sharper and more hostile, the prescribed punishments both in this world and the next become more severe.

The footnote to that last quote reads: "It is generally assumed by Western orientalists that the Arabic words 'lūwat' [*liwāṭ*?] ('sodomite' or 'sodomy') and 'lūṭī' (sodomite) are derived from the Arabic for 'Lot', but this seems [sic] extremely curious, since in all the Qur'ānic passages relating to Lot and the Sodomites it is made pellucidly clear that Lot was the one male in the city who did *not* involve himself in the sexual abuse of the angels."

The passage is misleading in several ways:

1. 'Sexual abuse' must be read as 'attempt to abuse sexually.'
2. Lot was not the only male who did not involve himself in this attempt. None of his *ahl*, his *familia* (including his male servants and clients) were involved,
3. Nowhere in the Qur'ān is the city (Sodom) named, the only way to name her inhabitants is "the people of Lot"—in the sense "the people to which Lot was sent by God," in the same way as the Arabs are "the people of Muḥammad." Thus

the 'Sodomites' could not be named after the city, but only after Lot.

4. Not *only* Western orientalists derive *liwāṭ* from *lūṭ*, but the Arab linguists, polyhistorians and commentators of the Qur'ān as well.[14]

Boswell goes on: "The persistence of 'lūṭī' as a derogation in Arabic literature should not be taken to reflect general social attitudes: its force in hostile comments is often more like that of 'cinaedus' than 'sodomite' . . . "

Boswell is not clear on the derogating force of Arabic words; that is why he uses the cautious 'often.' But he implies that the *meaning* (not just the 'force') of *lūṭī* is more like 'cinaedus,' whereas the opposite is true: *lūṭī* means roughly 'pedicator' (i.e., bugger)—'cinaedus' means 'effeminate singer, one who gets fucked (for money).'

The same footnote continues: "In rejecting the interpretation of Ibn Khaqan's nickname as 'pederast,' R. Dozy, the foremost lexicographer of Hispano-Arabic literature, comments that 'pederasty was so common among the Arabs at this time that it could not have been used as a term of reproach.'"

It is not "Ibn Khaqan's nickname" that is in question, but the nickname "Ibn H̱aqān." Boswell seems not to know the true meaning of "Ibn H̱aqān." As Dozy himself writes at the (partially quoted) entry of his dictionary: "an offensive nickname, a term of shocking rudeness . . . 'boy prostitute' . . . Ibn H̱aqān acquired this meaning when young Turks, the sons of the H̱aqāns who were educated at the Baghdad court, served to satisfy the abominable passions of the masters of this capital."[15] That 'pederast—bugger of boys'—could not be derogatory in the eyes of Ibn H̱aqān's contemporaries, but that 'berdache—boy prostitute' is highly negative, are facts that do not fit Boswell's "gay *Weltanschauung*."

STRANGE LOGIC

I fail to understand how the "dressing of pretty *girls* to look like pretty *boys*" shows that "*women* were obviously available to be appreciated as females."[16]

But even for those to whom that is 'obvious,' the phrasing "women who *participated* in this unusual form of transvestism" hides the not altogether insignificant fact that these women were slaves or servants/prostitutes, i.e., they were made to 'participate.'

In *Revolutions, Universals and Sexual Categories* Boswell claims that "When Saadia Gaon . . . discusses the desirability of 'passionate love' he apparently refers only to homosexual passion."[17] That is wrong: Saadia refers inter alia to Amnon's passion for Ṯamār (2. Samuel 13:15). Equally wrong is the assertion "That Saadia assumes the ubiquity of homosexual passion."

Creating the impression that the scholars of the Islamic world used the categories of homo- and heterosexuality, Boswell writes: "Saadia himself *cites* various theories about the determination of particular interests,"[18] whereas it would be correct to speak about Saadia citing and trying to refute various theories . . . Saadia does not share his opinions.

In the same context[19] Boswell writes, "Qusṭā discusses [the genetic causes of homosexuality] at some length, pp. 133-36." I cannot discover such a discussion on these pages—or anywhere else.

On page 19 of *Christianity* Boswell accuses a translator of having "transformed each story about gay love into a heterosexual romance by *altering the offending pronouns*," and thus shows that he knows little if anything about the Persian language (there are no different pronomina for male, female, and neutral). Yet he closes his discussions on the merits of different translations from Persian with this sentence: "There is of course no substitute for the original."

In note 100 (p. 196) he remarks critically: "This work is sometimes cited in French as *Un manuel hispanique de Hisba*, although the text is only in Arabic." But in note 101 (ibid.) he does exactly the same: he gives as the title of al-Maqqarī's purely Arabic work *Nafḥ aṭ-Tīb* (ed. R. Dozy, Leiden, 1855-66) only *Analectes sur l'histoire et la littérature des arabes d'Espagne*.

In note 106 he writes about the *faqi* of Valencia, without explaining what (or who) that is. I presume that a *faqīh* is meant, a jurisconsul, but in this case the phrase 'the *faqīh*' would be inappropriate, since there are several of them in bigger towns.

FAIRY TALES FROM 1001 NIGHTS

Boswell thinks it is still an open question "whether or not the *Nights* existed in any set form in the twelfth century"[20]; but it is certain that they already circulated in the ninth century in Arabic.[21]

Boswell: "It is extremely unlikely that the Arabic tale [of the dispute between the Man and the Learned Woman] in its present form could antedate 'Ganymed and Helene.'"[22] I discovered the tale in the writing of a 11th century author, aš-Šaizārī, a century earlier than 'Ganymede and Helena' (according to *Christ*. p. 258: twelfth century or later).

"Homosexuality occurs so frequently in the *Nights* that it would be impossible to cite even the major instances."[23] I myself count only about 20 and that includes very short ones (even the fifth of a sentence "in Tale 142 of the Nights," where according to Boswell[24] "it is mentioned as noteworthy that a male homosexual does not dislike woman," and where in reality a dyer is mentioned who enjoys both male and female: he is neither categorized as homo- nor as heterosexual but alluded to as 'bisexual' [digenitrop].

Boswell goes on: "in Night 419 a woman observes a man staring longingly at some boys . . . ."[25] In reality he stares at one boy, the woman's brother!

GAY BY BIRTH?

In this closing paragraph I want to demonstrate how misleading Boswell's presentation of his own and his opponents views in the controversy surrounding gay history can be. *Revolutions, Universals and Sexual Categories* purports to be a philosophical, impartial presentation of two possible attitudes toward homosexuality.[26] But while giving only the extreme view of the one camp, Boswell glosses over the more objectionable tenets of the other (instead of declaring, clearly 'we are born as homosexuals—we are homosexuals by nature,' he uses the learned adjectives 'inherent' and 'native'). I will first show how he presents his own camp's argument, then sum up his caricature of his opponents, and finally accurately state the position of a real opponent—myself.

Boswell: Humans are [from birth on] differentiated sexually . . . The category "heterosexuality" . . . describes a pattern of behavior inherent in human beings. All humans belong to one of two or more sexual categories, though external pressures or circumstances may induce individuals in a given society to pretend (or even to believe) that they belong to a category other than their native one.

Caricature: Socialization processes make the categories of sexual preference seem real to persons influenced by them. People consider themselves "homosexual" or "heterosexual" because they are induced to believe that humans are either "homosexual" or "heterosexual." Left to their own devices, without such socialization processes people would just be sexual.[27] The category "heterosexuality" . . . does not so much describe a pattern of behavior inherent in human beings as create and establish it.

All humans are polymorphously sexual, i.e., capable of erotic and sexual interaction with either gender. External accidents, such as social pressure, legal sanctions, religious beliefs, historical or personal circumstances determine the actual expression of each person's sexual feelings.

Schmitt: Adults are differentiated sexually. Certain socialization processes make humans into "homosexual" and "heterosexual" . . . If society/language offers the categories "heterosexuality" and "homosexuality," people will be labeled and perceive—possibly organize—themselves accordingly.

All humans are born amorphously sexual. Not external accidents but the essential process of nursing/caring/helping to grow up shape the sexual orientations, which are expressed under given social conditions.

NOTES

1. Chicago, 1980.
2. In Salmagundi 58/9, Saratoga Springs, N.Y., 1982.

3. *The Royal Treasure*, New Haven, Yale University Press, 1977 and *The Spain of Three Religions*.

4. *Christianity*. p. 194.

5. *Christianity*. p. 198.

6. *Christianity*. p. 194/5.

7. *Zwischenmännliche Sexualität und Erotik in der islamischen Gesellschaft. Bücher- und Personenliste zu Erotik/Sexualität zwischen Männern/Knaben im islamisch geprägten Vorderasien, Nordafrika und Südeuropa und deren Darstellung in Morgen- und Abendland*. This list comprises more than 30,000 items: titles of books, editions, pages with relevant passages, translations, secondary literature; dates of birth and death, country and profession. The book includes a complete index.

8. *Christianity*. p. 27 (emphasis added).

9. *Christianity*. p. 176.

10. Lisān ad-Dīn Ibn al-Haṭīb, *Kitāb Aʿmal al-aʿlam*, German in W.H., Islamische Geschichte Spaniens, Zürich, 1978, p. 408.

11. An image of graphic sexual import: the Arabic letters *lam* and *alif* were written together in a way that is here taken to suggest the insertion of one into the other. . . . (J. Boswell) (emphasis added).

12. Ibn Abdūn (12th century); Arabic text in *Journal asiatique*, 4.-6. 1934. p.241; French by Lévi-Provençal: *Seville musulmane au début du XIIè siècle*, Paris: Maisonneuve, 1947. p. 114.

13. Emphasis added.

14. The statement on the orientalists Henri Pérès and A.R. Nykl "neither is willing to admit the obvious implications of the texts he translates, and both express disgust at the thought that the literature could actually refer to the activities or feelings implied" is not supported by quotes or pages given.

15. *Christianity*. p. 195 (emphasis added).

16. Ibid. (emphasis added).

17. Boswell gives the title *Kitāb al-ʿAmanāt wa'l-Ictikhadāt* instead of . . . *Iʿtiqādāt*.

18. *Revolutions* p. 101.

19. *Revolutions* p. 103.

20. *Christianity*. p.257 n.56.

21. Nabia Abbott, *A Ninth-Century Fragment of the "Thousand Nights." New Light on the Early History of the Arabian Nights* in *Journal of Near Eastern Studies*, 1949.

22. *Christianity*. p.257.

23. Ibid.

24. *Revolutions* p. 102. There is no such thing as It in Tale 142 of the Calcutta edition of 1832-42, whereas in the best German translation (Enno Littmann, Insel-Verlag) it is Tale 155. In the popular translation (of the 'Breslau manuscript') by Gustav Weil it is the third from last story and there is no mentioning of the sexual liking of the dyer. For an English translation of The Story

of the Crafty Dalila see Richard Burton, *The Book of the Thousand Nights and a Night*, Benares, London, Kamasutra Society, 1885-88, vol. IV, p. 153 sq.

25. *Revolutions* p. 102, see Littmann vol. III 580.

26. Boswell does not even openly declare his view—one has to read between the lines.

27. There would be no human beings without socialization. Is Boswell of the opinion that there is in addition to the essential socialization a second one—a sexual one?

Islam

Maarten Schild

A major world religion, Islam stems from the preaching of the Prophet Muhammad in Arabia in the seventh century. It is based on the principle that the believer (or *muslim*) surrenders (Arabic: *islam*) to the will of the one and only God (Allah). God's will is expressed in Islamic law, consisting of a system of duties which every Muslim has to submit to by virtue of his belief. Islamic law, also known as the *Shari'ah* (path), forms a comprehensive code of behavior, a divinely ordained path of conduct that guides the Muslim in the practical expression of his religious conviction toward the goal of divine favor in paradise. Law is based on the *Koran*, the word of God as revealed to his Prophet, on the *Hadith*, which is a collection of the words and deeds attributed to the Prophet which are used as precedents, and on the interpretations of the Islamic jurists (*Ulama*).

BASIC FEATURES

A central theme is Islamic law and its theoretical attitude toward male homosexual behavior, and how this attitude relates to the way Muslims generally deal with such behavior in practice. It is difficult to speak of Islamic law in general, however, because of the differences of opinion among various Islamic law schools and sects (such as the Shi'a), while the same can be said of Islamic attitude in practice, as it varies in specific historical periods and regions. Even with a focus on material from the contemporary Middle East, an emphasis adopted in this article, general conclusions must be tentative.

Islam considers sexuality an absolutely normal and natural urge of every human being. Symbolic of this positive attitude is the important place sex is accorded in paradise, which will be the fulfillment of the spiritual and bodily self. Islamic representations of paradise depict a height of delights, with, among other things, girls whose virginity is continually renewed, immortal boys as beautiful as hidden pearls, perpetual erections and infinite orgasms. On earth, however, because of human imperfection, sex has a problematic side, which makes regulation necessary. Unregulated sex threatens the social order and leads to anarchy and chaos, and therefore has to be restricted to marriage. Marriage is a social obligation, and forms the basis of orderly society, giving expression to the divine harmony consisting of the complementarity of men and women. An essential and sacred part of marriage, sex is considered to be a tribute to divine will, an acknowledgement of God's kindness and generosity, and a fore-taste of the joys of paradise, which will sometimes lead to a renewal of his creation. Social order and the God-given harmony of life are threatened by the suppression of sexuality in celibacy and by sexual acts outside of marriage, heterosexual as well as homosexual. Celibacy is regarded as boring and unnatural, and rejected because it would inevitably lead to sinful feelings and to a knocking on forbidden doors. Sexual activity outside of marriage, adultery, is sharply condemned by Islamic law as a crime against humanity, which opens the door to many other shameful acts, and affects the reputation and property of the family, thereby disrupting the social fabric.

Homosexual behavior (*liwat*), i.e., sexual acts between members of the same sex, is considered to be adultery, being sex with an illicit partner. A person who performs such actions (*luti*) is regarded as extraordinarily corrupt, because he challenges the harmony of the sexes and topsyturvies God's creation: "Cursed are the men who behave effeminately, and cursed are the women who behave in a masculine way." Homosexual behavior is actually considered a revolt against God which violates the order of the world, and would be a source of evil and anarchy. The only remedy against such unnatural and sinful feelings is to fight and suppress them: "He who falls in love, conceals his passion, is chaste and patiently abstains, is forgiven by God and received into Paradise." Those who stubbornly persist in their behavior, however, await severe punishments, at least theoretically.

THE KORAN AND THE HADITH

In the Koran, homosexual behavior is explicitly condemned: "And as for the two of you who are guilty thereof, punish them both. If they repent and mend their ways, let them be. God is forgiving and merciful" (4:16). Homosexual behavior is further mentioned in the parable of the apostle Lot, which is repeatedly told in the Koran, and relates of the corrupted and evil-minded people of Lot's village, who transgressed consciously against the bounds of God. The behavior of these unbelievers was considered evil in general, their avarice led to inhospitality and robbery, which in turn led to the humiliation of strangers by mistreatment and rape. It was their homosexual behavior, however, that was seen as symptomatic of their attitudes, because it was regarded as "an abomination such as none in all the world has ever committed before." Obstinately refusing to accept God's message brought by Lot, the villagers were punished by God raining upon them "stones of heated clay" which killed them all and left their village ruined as a sign of the power of God for all to see. "The doings of the people of Lot" even became proverbial, alluding specifically to homosexual behavior, while the Arabic words for homosexual behavior and for a person who performs such actions both derive from Lot's name.

In the Hadith, homosexual behavior is condemned harshly: "Whenever a male mounts another male, the throne of God trembles," the angels look on in loathing and say: "Lord, why do you not command the earth to punish them and the heaven to rain stones on them?" God replies: "I am forebearing, nothing will escape me." Besides dreadful torments and humiliations in the world to come, homosexual behavior had to be punished on earth: "If you see two people who act like the people of Lot, then kill the active and the passive."

LEGAL SANCTIONS

The punishment that the Islamic jurists generally prescribe for adultery, and therefore also for homosexual behavior, is stoning to death for married people, and one hundred lashes for unmarried people. Persons who are married are punished more harshly because their behavior had severe consequences in regard to property and reputation, and would disrupt the family and the institution of marriage, both so important for the social order. The extravagant punishments that are prescribed are meant to have a deterring effect, and for that reason punishments are even carried out publicly.

Discouragement and repentance are considered more important than punishment, therefore the following conditions have to be met before condemnation is possible: Four adult muslims of the male sex, of unblemished integrity of character, have to swear that they have been eyewitnesses to the carnal act itself. Less than four witnesses will lead to a punishment of the witnesses themselves, while the false accuser will receive eighty lashes, because of slander. Perpetrators can only be condemned when adult, muslim, sane, and acting out of free will. A confession is sufficient for condemnation, if four times repeated. Before it is accepted, however, the judge has to point out to the accused the consequences of his confession, and the fact that repentance before the giving of testimony will be punished less harshly.

The fulfillment of all these conditions seems almost out of the question, leading to the conclusion that in practice it is only in very exceptional circumstances that persons are convicted and punished for adultery, and thus for homosexual behavior.

THEORY AND PRACTICE

Theoretically, homosexual behavior is sharply condemned by Islam, but in practice it is at present, and has been in the past, for the most part tolerantly treated and frequently occurring in countries where Islam predominates. The established societal norms and morals of Islam are accepted as unchangeable and respected by the majority of muslims, which does not imply, however, that they will or can conform to them in practice. Human beings are considered by Islam as imperfect, and are expected to make mistakes and consequently to sin. God is understanding of man's weaknesses, and when a person is sincere in his shame and shows repentance of his sinful behavior, he will be mercifully forgiven by God. In practice it is only public transgression of Islamic morals that is condemned, and therefore Islamic law stresses the role of eye-witnesses to an offense. The police are not allowed to go in search of possible sinners, who can only be caught red-handed, and not behind the "veil of decency" of their closed doors. In a way, concealment is advised, because to disclose a dreadful sin would be a sin in itself.

But it is not only condemnation by the law that can be avoided by secrecy, the same can be said of shame, a concept that plays an important part in the social role pattern of Islamic countries. Shame is engendered by what an individual thinks that others might think of him, and arises when public behavior is not according to the prescribed role, and therefore improper and disgraceful, bringing obloquy on the individual and tarnishing the reputation and standing of his family.

This emphasis on externals in Islamic law as well as in the social concept of shame, with its connivance in theoretically forbidden and shameful behavior, could be deemed hypocritical. But such a judgement would be beside the point, missing the essence of the entire matter, which is that in principle the validity of Islamic morals and of the social role pattern is confirmed by not openly resisting it, and it is just that which maintains the system as it is.

Kicking at the boundaries of permissibility by telling obscene and shocking anecdotes, sometimes expressed in literature but mostly in the conversation and speech of the people, has always been popular, but as long as it did not give rise to publicly unlawful behavior or to open resistance to morality, it posed no serious problem for the social order.

The generally tolerant attitude toward homosexual behavior in practice can partly be explained by the fact that it will usually take place discreetly. Moreover it does not have serious personal consequences such as, for example, heterosexual adultery would have. There is no question of abuse of possession (which a wife is of her husband) or of loss of honor and face of husband and family, while there fortunately exists no danger of pregnancy with all its consequences.

Practical tolerance therefore is the rule with respect to discreet homosexual behavior, but what about homosexuality?

Islamic law in theory only condemns homosexual acts and does not express itself on the subject of homosexuality. This is not in the least surprising, however, if we bear in mind that homosexuality is a western concept, crystallizing in the nineteenth century and stemming from the notion that sexual behavior is characteristic of someone's personality and identity, and therefore influences his behavior in general, leading to a certain lifestyle. Such a concept is essentially foreign to countries where Islam predominates, because there (sexual) behavior is not so much determined by personal preferences or someone's personality, as by a person's role and the circumstances in which he finds himself. Generally speaking, a person behaves in a particular situation as much as possible according to the social role pattern that prescribes whether a certain kind of behavior in that situation is proper or not. He conforms to this, because otherwise he would bring shame on himself and his family, and lose face and honor. For that reason it is, for example, not particularly important if a sexual act is homo- or heterosexual, but rather which role is performed (active, as is proper for a man, or passive, like a woman), and if the act has social consequences or not. Therefore, concepts like homo- and heterosexuality make no sense in cultures like these. Such contemporary western principles as "I am a homosexual, and thus I do not marry" are laughed at, because a person has to comply with his role, and therefore is expected to marry and beget children. As long as he maintains his role in public, his private preferences and idiosyncracies are nobody's business but his own, that is if he is discrete about them, and harms no one.

THE REPRESSION IN IRAN

What, then, of the executions of homosexuals in Iran between 1979 and 1984? The problem here is a confusion of terms, because the "homosexuality" meant in Iran is far different from the western concept of it. In Iran "homosexuality" has become a negative label, as it has in other Islamic countries, but fortunately with less extreme consequences. The label "homosexuality" refers to behavior that clashes with the God-given order of society and with the social role pattern; it is behavior that violates public decency, and is moreover seen as a typical example of western decadence. "Homosexuality" refers specifically to passive homosexual behavior, which is considered particularly objectionable, because it turns God's creation topsyturvy, and threatens the God-given harmony between men and women, which is reflected in the social role pattern. A man who plays the active, penetrator role in a homosexual act behaves like a man, and is therefore not considered "homosexual." Passive homosexual behavior, however, implies being penetrated like a woman, and is considered to be extremely scandalous and humiliating for a man, because it is feminine behavior. Deviant behavior like this was in olden times viewed as abnormal and unnatural, and sometimes even characterized as an illness, because it was incomprehensible that a man could voluntarily choose to be dishonored and debased in the role of a woman. More common is the belief that sexual behavior that deviates from the norm causes illness, a notion soon to be confirmed by the appearance of AIDS.

Another myth that influences the negative labeling of "homosexuality" is that of the foreignness of sexually deviant behavior. In past centuries the Arabs ascribed homosexual behavior to Persian influence, and nowadays it is mostly regarded as originating from the West—a rather paradoxical viewpoint, because it used to be the other way around. Western society is viewed as shameless and depraved, permissiveness making license public and ultimately leading to social chaos. "Homosexuality" epitomizes this western decadence, this "unbridled riot of wantonness."

Finally, "homosexuality" also refers to the public transgression of morals, the conscious refusal to hide behind the veil of secrecy, and thus openly challenging established norms and values. As is the story of Lot, it is today "homosexuality" that has become symptomatic of evil behavior in general. "Homosexuality" would inevitably lead to chaos and decay, and therefore "homosexuals" are considered as antisocial, and as a threat to social order. Ayatollah Khomeini (who died in 1989) alluded to this idea, asserting that "homosexuals" had to be exterminated because they were parasites and corruptors of the nation by spreading the "stain of wickedness." "Homosexuality" not only is seen as evil in itself, but provides a convenient label for stigmatizing bad people in general. This broad-gauge definition underpinned what happened in Iran, where "homosexuality" was often deployed as a generic label to be applied at will to persons adjudged criminals, whether rightly or wrongly. It did not matter much what they did, it was enough to know that they were antisocial and therefore evil. In this way, for example, political opponents could be eliminated without any legal justification. In times of crisis especially, when the need for security is strong, public morals tend to become more severe, and deviant behavior that was once ignored is repressed. Moreover, in a period of political, economic, and social instability, internal chaos will often be blamed on outsiders and foreigners.

But what occurred in Iran is certainly not typical of the attitude toward homosexual behavior in the whole spectrum of Islamic countries. Even in Iran it may be regarded as exceptional. The executions of "homosexuals" took place in an atmosphere of revolutionary turbulence, with strong reactionary and antiwestern accents that led to excesses and an overall atmosphere of terror. Yet the foundation of such extremes is probably present in all Islamic countries, and stems from a negative attitude toward passive homosexual behavior, couples with a rejection of western morality and condemnation of public indecency. Therefore "homosexuality" is rejected. In practice homosexual behavior is usually treated tolerantly as long as it is discrete and harms no one. This tolerance was well characterized by the words of an unknown Arab poet: "As the boy looked at it, my thing moved, and he whispered: 'It is splendid! Do let me try its love making.' I answered 'Such an act is reprehended, in fact many people call it unlawful.' He said: 'Oh them; oh them! With me all things are lawful.' And I was too polite to disobey."

LESBIANISM

Of female same-sex behavior (*musahaqa*) almost nothing is known. Islamic law considers it sex outside of marriage and therefore as adultery, with all the consequences already described. Yet because no penetration takes place, punishment is theoretically limited to one hundred lashes. In practice lesbian behavior is regarded as relatively unimportant, because it usually takes place discreetly.

BIBLIOGRAPHY

Abdelwahab Bouhdiba, *Sexuality in Islam*, trans. A. Sheridan, London: Routledge & Kegan Paul, 1985.

C. H. Bousquet, *L'éthique sexuelle de l'Islam*, Paris: Maisonneuve, 1966.

Madelaine Farah, *Marriage and Sexuality in Islam: A Translation of al Ghazzali's Book on the Etiquette of Marriage*, Salt Lake City: University of Utah Press, 1984.

Gabrielle Mandel, *Islamische Erotik*, Fribourg: Liber, 1983.

Basim F. Musallam, *Sex and Society in Islam: Birth Control before the Nineteenth Century*, 1983.

A. L. al Sayyid Marsot, *Society and the Sexes in Medieval Islam*, Malibu, CA: Undena, 1979.

Man of Ashes: A Film Review

Jehoeda Sofer

For his debut film, the Tunisian director Nouri Bouzid chose topics rarely dealt with in Arabic films: sexuality, manliness, and arranged marriage. In 1966/67 Bouzid worked for Tunisian television and has been an assistant director in 15 films, including *Raiders of the Lost Ark* produced by Steven Spielberg. In 1986 "Man of Ashes" attracted much attention at the Cannes Film Festival and was crowned at the Eleventh Carthage Film Festival.[1] It was acclaimed as the most important Arab film.[2]

The film tells the story of Hachemi, (Imed Maalal) a young woodcarver in the provincial town of Sfax, on the eve of his marriage to a girl chosen by his parents. Everything is ready for the ceremony, but Hachemi himself is not. His problem is not so much that he does not know the bride, but traumatic memories: at the age of 10, he and his friend Farfat (Khaled Ksouri) were raped by their master, the carpenter Ameur.

While the women are preparing for the wedding and the men are sitting in the café, Hachemi flees to Farfat in order to sort out the past. The wedding has to be cancelled. In Arab society where the family forms a central element, this is a shame that damages not only Hachemi's reputation, but also that of his whole family.

Farfat, an outsider, a rebel who dreams of the opportunities of the big city, is thrown out of the house by his father. Someone wrote the stigmatizing graffito "Farfat is not a man" on the wall. Azouez, a childhood friend of Hachemi and Farfat, expresses his doubts about their manliness. He takes them to a brothel, an initiation, a test for the wedding night. Hachemi's whore is very kind: He has no problem performing. It is a reassuring, relaxing experience for the pretty young man with bright, almost hairless skin—very smooth for a man. But Farfat feels he has to prove his masculinity in another way. He must free himself from the writing on the wall. He kills Ameur with a knife. As the film ends, we see him chased by the police and run down by a train.

Another theme of the film is the patriarch. Bouzid shows the heavy emotional burden of the relations between father and son in Arab society. The powerful father figure appears in three forms: the biological father and head of the family; the Jewish teacher and musician Levy, who for Hachemi embodies wisdom; and Ameur the master and rapist.

The only emancipated woman in the film is the fascinating madam of the brothel. For Bouzid she symbolizes the positive aspects of traditional life, full of calm beauty, but definitely belonging to the past.

No one in the film can be considered "gay". Homosexuality is never openly discussed, but sex between males and machismo are central subjects in the film, as are the loss of innocence and the irreparable break between childhood and adulthood. Friendship between males is another important theme. The friendship between the three boys is threatened by the marriage; it is the break with childhood. It is expressed in the film by the Arabic saying: "Marriage buries man's past." They are forced to confront their problems without the help of friends. What emerges from this social confrontation is a man of ashes. *Man of Ashes* is a serious attempt to deal with the psychology of the Arab man and frustration of the young generation.

NOTES

1. Arabic film title: *Rih essed*. Director Nouri Bouzid. Actors, Imed Maalal (Hachemi), Khaled Ksouri, Habib Belhadi, Wassila Shawki. Tunisia, 1986. 109 minutes.

2. Hédi Khélil, Matière, mémoire et regard in Sociétés No 28 (4. 1990), pp. 27–30.

Bibliography

Benard, Cheryl, and Schlaffer, Edit. *Die Grenzen des Geschlechts*. Reinbeck: Rowohlt, 1984.

Būhdība, ʿAbdalwahhāb. "The Child and the Mother in Arab-Muslim Society." *Psychological Dimensions* (L. Carl Brown, ed.), Princeton, 1977.

Djait, Hichem. *La Personalité et le devenir arabo-islamique*. Paris, Seuil, 1974.

Guttari, Felix (ed.). *Trois milliardes de pervers. Arabes et pédés*. Paris, 1973.

Rosenthal, Frank. "Ar-Rāzi on the Hidden Illness." *Bulletin of the History of Medicine*, 52, 1978.

Šarabī, Hišam Bašir. *Muqqadima li-dīrasat al-muğtamaʿal-ʿarabī*. Bairūt, 1975.

Sayyid-Marsot, A. Lutfi (ed.). *Society and the Sexes in Medieval Islam*. Malibu: Udena, 1977 (Sixth G. Levy della Vida Bi-annual Conference). See especially the articles by James A. Bellamy and S. D. Goitein.

Schiffauer, W. *Die Gewalt der Ehre*. Frankfurt: Suhrkamp, 1983.

Slater, Philip E. *The Glory of Hera*. Boston: Beacon, 1969.

Wikan, Unni. *Behind the Veil in Arabia: Woman in Oman*. Baltimore: Johns Hopkins University Press, 1982.

About the Contributors

Andreas Eppink (b.1946) studied psychology (PhD) and anthropology at the University of Amsterdam with field work in Morocco and specialized in cross-cultural communication, with special interest in Mediterranean and Arab cultures. Author of several books and articles, he works as a psychotherapist.

Thijs Janssen (b.1961) studied cultural anthropology at the Catholic University of Nijmegen (the Netherlands). His doctoral thesis was about the images of homosexual behavior in Turkey (1987).

Badruddin Khan is a gay man of Pakistani origin now living in Toronto.

Gary B. MacDonald lived and worked in Morocco, Syria, Lebanon, Jordan and all of the Arabian Peninsula countries from 1977-1984. From 1984-1987 he created and was the first director of the AIDS Action Council, a non-profit advocacy organization representing all U.S. community organizations providing AIDS education and services. Since 1987, he has provided policy and management support to Latin American and Asian governments as they plan and implement national AIDS prevention programs.

Gianni De Martino hails from South Italy (Angri, Salerno) and lives in Milano. He is founder and director of the quarterly "Mandala," chief-editor of "Mundo Beat," and contributor to many journals and to the book *Morocco, Nord Africa*. Together with George Lapassade he edited *Saggio Sulla France* (1980). He visits the Maġreb regularly.

Mehmet Ümit Necef (b.1952) was born in Turkey and studied cultural sociology at the University of Copenhagen. He has written papers on Islām's role in Turkey, homosexuality, and women's questions.

Charles Pellat (b.1914) was born in Algeria. He studied literature at the University of Bordeaux (France) and Algiers (PhD) and taught at the Ecole Nationale de Langues Orientales Vivantes (1951-56) and at the Sorbonne (1956-78). He is one of the editors of the *Encyclopaedia of Islam*, a member of the Academie des Sciences d'oûtre-mer, member correspondent at the Academie Indienne de Langue Arabe, and a member of the Academie des Inscriptions et Belle-lettres. His publications include: *Langue et Litterature arabes* (1952), *l'Arabe Vivant* (1952), *Le Milieu basrien et la formation de Ǧāḥiz* (1953), *Textes berbères* (1955), and *Ibn Shuhayd* (1963). He has won prizes of the Academie des inscriptions et belles-lettres (1953) and the Academie francaise (1953).

David Reed is a freelance writer now living in New York (and never again in Tehran).

Maarten Schild studied History at the University of Utrecht. His main subject was the contemporary history of the Middle East. He is currently working as a trainer in communications and informal skills at the University of Wageningen. He wrote his doctoral thesis on *Homosexual Behavior and Islam in the Middle East* and has published articles and given lectures on the subject. His publications in English include *The Irresistible Beauty of Boys: Middle Eastern Attitudes About Boy-Love* and several articles for the *Encyclopedia of Homosexuality*.

Index